Practical Yacht Navigator

At sea, but where?

Practical Yacht Navigator

Kenneth Wilkes

Fifth edition

NAUTICAL

First published in Great Britain 1987 by
NAUTICAL BOOKS
an imprint of A & C Black (Publishers) Ltd
35 Bedford Row,
London WC1R 4JH

First edition 1973
Second edition 1974
Reprinted 1975
Third edition 1979
Reprinted 1981
Fourth edition 1985
Fifth edition 1987

ISBN 0 7136 5700 6

Filmset and printed by
BAS Printers Limited, Over Wallop, Hampshire

Contents

In chapter 19 will be found details of navigational ability required for the Royal Yachting Association Yachtmaster Offshore Certificate and a key to chapters throughout this book against the syllabus.

Line drawings:
Bill Streets

Log book examples:
Jillian Andrew

Cover design: Dick Everitt
Cover photograph of Bridget Webb on board *Jacobite* by Patrick Roach
Photographs by Peter Johnson except for
Raymond Austen page 25,
J. H. Bottrell 26
Trinity House 28, 29,
Kelvin Hughes 150, 151, 152,
EMI, Marine 152,
Brookes and Gatehouse 56,
Racal Decca Marine 140,
Seafarer Navigation International 58, 59,
Thomas Walker and Son 142

Reproductions on page 22, 106, 107, 109, 110 are with the sanction of the Controller of H.M. Stationery Office and the Hydrographer of the Navy.

Extract from Burton's Nautical Tables by permission of George Philip and Son Ltd.

1. Lost on the Water

Since the first edition of this book was published in 1973, yacht navigation has changed immensely. In a suitably equipped vessel a member of the crew has only to read off at the chart table, or even in the cockpit, the latitude and longitude to an accuracy of a boat's length or so. The actual system depends on where in the world the yacht is and what aids are installed, but electronic devices now solve nearly all basic navigational queries.

Whether it is still necessary to learn the old systems is now questioned. One can however immediately think of circumstances where electronic aids cannot help. These include complete power failure—not so rare in a sailing boat or disabled motor boat—as well as instrument failure or loss of the relevant antenna. Then there is the inadvisability of relying on a single navigational aid and the ability to back it up with basic skills. Further the navigator may be invited aboard a small yacht with no such electronics, or be caught unexpectedly offshore after dark (perhaps due to calm) or in bad visibility in a boat intended mainly for day sailing. Simplest of all the owner may not have any such aids, be unable to afford them, or not wish to have them, preferring to navigate, just as he prefers to use sails, which no commercial vessel would consider anyway (with certain noted exceptions).

This book is concerned with coastal navigation and passage making on relatively short sea crossings out of sight of land, say not more than 250 nautical miles. For longer distances out of sight of terrestrial aids other methods (the sextant, satellite navigation) are required and a companion volume, *Ocean Yacht Navigator*, deals with these. Navigation in yachts is essentially practical and big ship methods or pure classroom work cannot succeed. A good test of ability is to imagine yourself asleep below in a yacht, which the owner has taken out for a day sail. You slept longer than expected until he wakes you to say 'Can you help. We have not been taking much notice of where we are and quite frankly, we are a bit lost!' You have compass, charts and pilot books and you need to recover the situation. A number of tasks would immediately have to be performed, as you got control of the situation—the new navigator.

My own first attempt at a passage out of sight of land did not actually involve negligence, though perhaps ignorance. It was just the sort of run that scores of yachts make for the first time every season: a simple run of 60 miles from Poole Harbour to Cherbourg across the English Channel. I pencilled a line on the chart joining these two places. This gave me a course to steer on the the boat's compass. The distance seemed rather difficult to calculate because the chart did not have a scale of miles to the inch like a road map. Someone in the yacht club said that it was best to sail by night because lighthouses flashed out, making it easy to find where you were. I memorized the characteristics of three prominent lighthouses.

practical yacht navigator

Off we went on a reach. About 0200—much sooner than I had expected—a flashing light appeared dead ahead. It was flashing every five seconds. This was the characteristic of Cap de la Hague, some 12 miles to the west of my destination. The only problem was that the colour of the light was red, while Cap de la Hague is white. I felt sure my red light must be at Cherbourg so I searched round there on the chart by a dim torch light, but nowhere near Cherbourg could I find a red light flashing every 5 secs. Almost at once I heard the sound of breaking water on all sides. I then did probably the only sensible thing I did that night, I stood out to sea and hove-to. By daylight I could clearly see the Barfleur lighthouse at the eastern end of the Cherbourg peninsula, and could now find my red flashing 5 sec. light—Cap Levi—some 5 miles to the east of Cherbourg. During the night we had stood in to Cap Levi and the broken water I had heard was the fast east-going tide rushing over shoal rocks, fortunately then well below the surface. The weather had remained quiet and we had come to no harm, but we had many hours sailing to reach Cherbourg. Had the weather turned rough or visibility deteriorated we might have been in serious trouble.

Shortly after, I met a man who told me of a trip he had made from Cherbourg back to the Solent. He mistook Anvil Point lighthouse light for St. Catherine's light and finished up in Weymouth, about 25 miles to the west of his destination. Again, he came to no harm as the weather was settled and visibility good, but it could well have been otherwise if conditions had turned bad.

Incidents of this sort probably happen many times every season. With fine weather—and a bit of luck—no damage is done but a lot of time may be wasted. But if the weather turns foul, then the trouble starts. At best a very anxious time is had by all, and at worst disaster may strike. Many rescues by lifeboat are a result of navigation which has gone haywire.

The yachtsman does not have to learn navigation like a merchant navy officer, but his navigational problems are basically the same. Courses of study and examinations suitable for the yachtsman are discussed in Chapter 19. But it is not at all necessary to take these to gain a grasp of navigational matters. It is practical ability that he needs.

A cursory glance at a text book on navigation may give the impression that the subject is difficult and calls for a lot of mathematics and complex calculations. In fact, navigation is based on common sense and a little very elementary geometry. Early sailors managed to navigate without the advantage of study—they were able to do so by observation of the results of wind and tide, by deductions based on what they saw, and by amassing experience. All that a text book can do is to point out the problems, and indicate solutions: this reduces the time required to amass experience.

Now here is an important point. Most people soon master the principles in any navigation problem quite quickly, but fail to reach the correct answer. It is because they are inaccurate. They make mistakes in simple addition or subtraction, add when they should subtract, or pick up the wrong figure from a table. More students fail examinations by making silly, simple mistakes than by not knowing the principles involved. The trouble is that this happens more often at sea, than when practising on land.

It may be argued that a degree or so error in a course does not matter as one can seldom steer to that accuracy. This is true. But if one is careless an error is just as likely to be 10° as 1°—and it then becomes serious if not dangerous. It is particularly important to ensure that signs are right—plus or minus—since an error in the sign produces an error of double the figure. If a variation of 10° W is applied the wrong way the course will be 20° wrong—which makes 20 miles error on a 60 mile passage.

The golden rule which it is most strongly recommended should be followed in every navigation problem is:

Check every figure, and every sign (+ or −), every 'name'—N or S, E or W.

Check every addition and subtraction (check subtraction by 'adding back')

Tick every sign and figure when checked.

Do not USE any answer till every figure has been ticked as checked.

This procedure should be followed when working out exercises at home or at sea, and when working 'for real'. It is a temptation to press on with calculations—particularly at sea—to get a speedy answer, without 'wasting time' checking. But if the checking is done while the table-book or tidal atlas, or whatever, is open and to hand, it only takes a moment, and will save a lot of unnecessary work in re-calculating if the first answer is obviously wrong. If it is not obviously wrong, possibly hours of unnecessary sailing may be involved, and even danger incurred, all through omitting to check at each stage.

So, right from the start, make it routine to check and tick every figure and calculation.

Your work will be made easier, and the risk of error reduced, if you write clearly and neatly, and do not omit captions. Do not overwrite a wrong figure, but cross it out and put the new figure clearly. By 'caption' is meant the meaning of what has just been written—e.g. water track 210° true.

There is no reason why you should not use your own abbreviations, provided you know exactly what they mean, e.g. water tk. 210° T'. Many a mistake has been made by the wrong figure being picked up, or misunderstood.

When writing some figures down which need subtraction or addition, ensure they are written plumb under each other. Again this speeds the work and helps accuracy.

These may seem obvious or trivial points, but experience shows that they pay handsome dividends. Good navigation calls for meticulous attention to detail and neat, accurate writing more than any high degree of technical ability.

Pilotage

Pilotage is a name given to such things as directing a vessel into or out of a harbour, estuary or river. Position and direction are ascertained by eye using local knowledge or chart, coupled with use of the compass, particularly in poor visibility or by night. There is no time for, and little necessity for, plotting the ship's course on the chart, the operation calling for knowledge of the position in relation to the channel, of buoys and other navigational marks, and for the ability to identify these objects as seen.

In many designated 'Pilotage' areas regulations require all commercial vessels (or vessels over a stated tonnage) to employ a certificated pilot. Yachts are not obliged to carry pilots (except in a very few specific places).

A yachtsman sailing say from Portsmouth to Yarmouth, Isle of Wight would use pilotage, determining his course by reference to buoys and landmarks. He would not require to pre-determine courses to steer nor to plot his position on the chart in daylight and normal weather. Nevertheless, many of the features of navigation which are essential on a longer passage may be used, and in

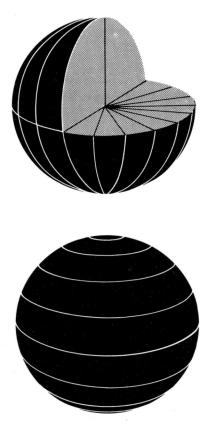

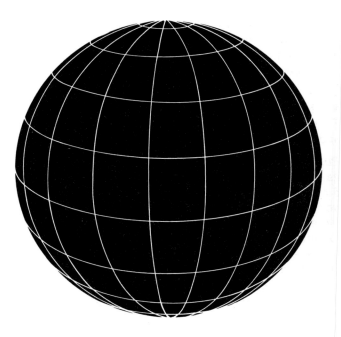

Fig 1. This is what meridians are. Known, too, as longitude. They are by definition 'great circles'.

Fig 2. Parallels of latitude.

Fig 3. When these are combined, the result is a natural system of reference over the seas of the world, in terms of latitude and longitude.

poor visibility or at night may be necessary.

Pilotage calls for thorough knowledge of the buoyage systems, the proper use of the echo sounder (or leadline). The direction of tidal streams, the use of leading lights and marks, port entry signals and the recognition of navigational marks by their lights at night is also necessary. These are all dealt with later.

Navigation as a general subject

There are some words used over and over again and their explanation is as follows:

Position. A position can be described in terms of its relationship to a stated object, e.g. 'position, 5 miles south of Beachy Head lighthouse'. When not close to an easily identified object, it may be more precisely described by its latitude and longitude of which more in a minute.

There are 360 degrees (360°) in a circle, 60 minutes (60') in a degree. Fractions of a minute of arc are recorded in decimals, e.g. $50° 25\frac{1}{2}$ being written 50°25'·5

The equator is a great circle girding the earth exactly midway between north and south geographic poles. A straight line which passes through both the north and south geographical pole is a meridian. It cuts the equator at right angles, and is half a great circle (a circle which cuts the centre of the earth). The meridian which passes through Greenwich is termed the prime meridian, and is named 0°.

Any number of meridians can be drawn, at any desired angular distance from the prime meridian measured either at the centre of the earth, along the equator, or at either pole (all give the same figure). Any meridian is named by this angle, in degrees and minutes, and is named east or west, and can be any angle up to 180° E or 180° W. (Fig 1.)

A parallel of latitude is a line drawn parallel to the equator and girding the earth. Any number of parallels of latitude can be drawn, cutting every meridian at right angles, and each passing through a given point on any meridian measured from the equator along a meridian. The angular distance of any parallel of latitude is measured along a meridian, or at the centre of the earth, from the equator towards either pole, and is named north or south, and any angle up to 90°. (Fig 2.)

The latitude of a position is therefore stated as being a given number of degrees and minutes north or south of the equator, measured along the meridian on which it lies. (Fig 3.)

Its longitude is given as the degrees and minutes which the meridian on which it lies is east or west of the prime meridian, 0° (Greenwich meridian).

Direction. A direction in the business of navigating can be described as a line between the observer and an object, or between two objects or positions. The direction of an object is defined in terms of the angle between the object and some 'datum' line. The direction of one object or position from another position, or from the observer, is therefore the commonly used 'bearing'.

The meridians on a chart all run true north and south—they join the two poles. If the angle between the line representing a bearing and a meridian is measured, this is a true bearing. Bearings are normally measured in 360° notation, measuring the angle from true north (the meridian, or a line parallel to it) clockwise round to the bearing. A bearing in degrees may therefore be anything from 0 to 359 (always measured clockwise), and may be designated true bearing by the suffix T, e.g. 040°T. (Fig 4.) See page 14.

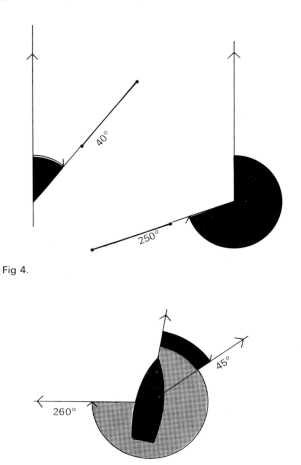

Fig 4.

Fig 5.

Fig 4. Bearings are given clockwise in degrees. Normally three digits are used, e.g. 040°

Fig 5. A relative bearing. Top shows relative bearings from 'ship's head' of 45° and 260°. Bottom shows bearings from 'ship's head'; in this case, 90° to starboard, 45° to port.

If the bearing is measured in relation to the direction of north as shown by a magnetic compass, then this will usually differ from the true bearing because compass north usually differs from true (geographic) north. A compass bearing is always shown with the suffix C, e.g. 090° C. (see Chapter 5).

A bearing which is related to the direction of the yacht's head (the direction she is going) is called a relative bearing. Used often to give a quick indication of a general direction, it does not require the observer to refer to the compass, e.g. 'vessel seen 45° on port bow', or 'buoy seen 90° on starboard bow, or abeam to starboard'. The Navy gives relative bearings in degrees and colour, green to starboard, red to port, e.g. 'Red 45' indicates 45° from dead ahead to port. 'Green 90' indicates 90° from dead ahead to starboard. (Fig 5.)

Distance. All distances are measured in nautical (or sea) miles. The nautical mile is divided into 10 cables, normally shown as decimals of a mile, 2 miles 4 cables is written 2·4 M. The nautical mile is, by definition, the distance of one minute of arc measured along a meridian. As the earth is not a perfect sphere, this distance varies between 1843 metres at the equator and 1862 metres at the pole, but for practical purposes the average is now taken as a mean of 1852 m (6076 ft). The cable is a fraction over 200 yards.

Note that the nautical mile is appreciably longer than the statute mile of 5 280 feet (over 15 per cent), which is an arbitrary measurement fixed in the sixteenth century.

Speed
The unit used is always the knot, (abbreviations kn or K), which is one nautical mile in one hour.

Depths
The old unit of depth is the fathom (fm), being 6 feet. Fractions are shown as fathoms and feet. Thus 7_4 represents 7 fms 4 ft.

The new unit, used on British charts as they are reprinted, and on most foreign charts, is the metre (m). Fractions are shown in decimetres or decimals of a metre. Thus 8_7 indicates 8.7 metres.

Note : small m denotes metres
        capital M denotes nautical miles.
This may well apply to the same object when navigating, for instance a lightship may be 21m high and visible 14M away.

Bearings on charts and lists of lights
All bearings shown with no suffix (e.g. 'lights in line bearing 174°') are true bearings (from seaward). All Admiralty charts show true bearings, without the suffix T, but many 'yachtsman's' charts and pilot books show bearings and courses magnetic (e.g. 095° M). To guard against error, it is advisable to put T against all true bearings which you write down, to distinguish clearly from those which may be magnetic or compass. This is explained more fully in Chapter 5.

2. The Mariner's Map

A chart is a mariner's map. It shows him where it is safe for him to sail—and more important—shows where it is not. It shows the various ports and harbours and their positions relative to each other so that he can shape a course from one to another. A mass of 'signposts' in the form of landmarks are given so that he can fix his position in relation to them. The shape of the coastal hills, cliffs, sand dunes and the general 'picture' of the coast are all shown. The depths of water and even the nature of the sea bed are given. So you can see a chart is far more than simply a map, and enables the navigator to form an accurate picture of the area shown.

Once the knack of 'reading' a chart is acquired, the yachtsman can visualize even a strange area in advance. He knows what to expect before he gets there, knows where the dangers lie, where the safe channels are, and can navigate in confidence. Like a good book, the more one reads it the more one knows about the subject. But a chart contains so much information that quite a lot of it has to be written in a form of shorthand. Much of this takes the form of symbols which indicate their meaning by their shapes. Other data are given by abbreviations or initials, which are easily remembered after a little practice.

A very clear understanding of what a chart shows is important for safe navigation. Each symbol and abbreviation has one precise meaning and only one meaning, and one has to learn to be extremely careful to recognize the exact message being conveyed. This applies particularly to the shape and colour of buoys shown, the precise type of light of a given lighthouse, and so on. This only comes with practice, and the reader is recommended to study a chart or charts in detail, identifying every mark or symbol and checking with the list of symbols and forms given in publications such as:

Admiralty Publication No. 5011. Symbols and Abbreviations.

Types of chart

Charts may be broadly classified between

1. Navigational charts for keeping a track of a ship's position and for determining courses to be steered.

2. Non-Navigational charts for special purposes, such as

(a) Routeing charts showing details of winds, weather, principal shipping routes.
(b) Lattice charts for position finding by radio aids.
(c) Radio beacon charts.
(d) Tidal stream charts and atlases.

(e) Charts of isogonic variation and other specialized information.

Navigational charts

Admiralty charts are published by the Hydrographic Department, Ministry of Defence. Coverage is worldwide. They are available from official chart agents in most ports and large cities in U.K. and abroad. Their disadvantage for the smaller yacht is their size. The Hydrographic Department publishes a full catalogue showing the area covered by each sheet, and also lists various Admirality sailing directions or 'Pilots', lists of lights, fog signals, radio signals, and other books. The catalogue is valuable for selecting the charts required for any passage. An abbreviated catalogue (NP 91) is also available listing charts covering the British Isles and adjacent continental waters, of particular value to yachtsmen in the U.K. and Ireland.

Other countries produce good charts, particularly large-scale charts of their local waters.

Imray Laurie Norie & Wilson Ltd., produce a 'Y' series of charts on small format sheets, ideal for craft where space is limited. The series contains some smaller scale coastal charts but generally gives large scale coverage to estuaries and rivers. They also produce a 'C' series designed for cruising and in most cases they include harbour plans. Both series are coloured and available laminated in plastic.

Barnacle Marine Ltd. produce Stanford's charts. These include the English Channel, part of the East Coast including rivers and estuaries, the Bristol Channel and the North Brittany coast. There are useful pilotage notes on the back of these coloured charts and they are available printed on waterproof paper called *Allweather* charts.

Chart projections

The earth is an 'oblate spheroid', that is, a sphere

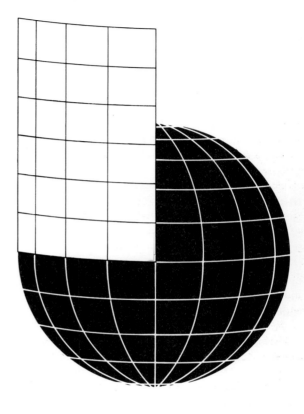

Fig 6.   For navigation we need a flat chart, but the earth is roughly spherical. So every attempt to make a chart is a compromise.

slightly flattened at top and bottom. The cartographer is faced with the problem of reproducing the surface of this sphere, or a portion of it, on a flat piece of paper. (Fig 6.). It is clearly impossible to flatten out an orange skin—or a large piece of one—without either cutting it or stretching it in some way. The same applies to a section of the earth's surface. Whatever he does, the cartographer is bound to distort the area depicted in some ways. There are several methods of 'projecting' the earth's curved surface on to a flat plane. The principal projections used in sea navigation are Mercator's projection and the gnomonic projection.

Mercator projection

On a sphere (the earth) the (horizontal) parallels of latitude are lines all parallel to the equator and thus to each other, and are equally spaced. But the (vertical) meridians, though also straight and cutting each parallel of latitude at right angles, all meet at the poles and are therefore tapering together as they approach either pole.

To represent a section of the globe on a flat surface, the cartographer draws his meridians all vertical and parallel to each other, and spaced *equally* apart. To prevent distortion of the *shapes* of the land, he expands the distance between parallels of latitude to correspond with the amount he has pulled the meridians apart to make them parallel. Thus, while the *shape* of each part of a chart is correct, the *scale* varies gradually between top and bottom of the chart. (Fig 7.). The practical effects of this are :

(a) A straight line on a Mercator chart cuts each meridian at the same angle, so that true bearings of the line will remain unchanged along its length.
(b) The shortest distance between two points on a sphere is a portion of a Great Circle (a circle whose plane cuts the centre of the earth). This

will appear as a curved line on a Mercator chart, bowed away from the equator.
(c) Distances on the chart must be scaled off from the *latitude* scale (on vertical edges of the chart), and level with the part being measured as the scale varies. Check this by placing the dividers on, say, 10' of latitude near the bottom of the chart. Then, without disturbing the dividers, place them on the same scale towards the top of the chart. It will at once be apparent that the space between 10' on the chart towards the top is greater than it was at the bottom, if the chart is of the northern hemisphere (or less if of the southern hemisphere).

A straight line between two points on a Mercator chart is called a rhumb line. Although not the shortest distance between the two points, there is negligible difference between this and a Great Circle course if the distance is less than about 500 miles, in latitudes less than about 60° N or S, and can safely be disregarded for coastal navigation. In practice, all coastal and short passages are laid off on the chart as rhumb lines or straight lines on a Mercator chart. (Fig 8.)

Gnomonic projection

Charts on the Gnomonic Projection are only used for very high latitudes (polar charts), for plotting long-distance Great Circle tracks, and other special purposes. The meridians radiate out from the nearer pole, and the parallels of latitude appear as circumferences or arcs of circles whose centres are at the nearer pole. On these charts a Great Circle track appears as a straight line, cutting each meridian at a different angle, while a rhumb line would appear as a curved line, bowed from the nearer pole. (Fig 9.)

A shipmaster, requiring to shape a great circle course between two ports a thousand or more miles apart so as to minimize his mileage would

Fig 7. Flat chart actually represents surface of sphere.

Fig 8. In Mercator projection, a course can be laid off as a straight line but distances are distorted from north to south. Curved line represents great circle. This is the projection of an 'ordinary chart'.

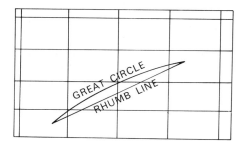

Fig 9. Gnomonic projection : great circle is now represented by straight line, but straight course on Mercator now becomes curved.

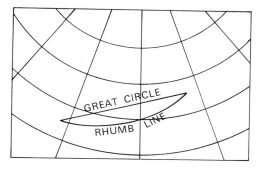

use a gnomonic chart. He would draw in a straight line between the ports, pick up the latitude and longitude of a series of points along this line, and transfer these points to a mercator chart. Joining these points would produce a series of short straight lines bending round. He could then determine the positions where an alteration of course should be made to maintain his position along the great circle line. A yacht on a long passage, whether sail or power, seldom sails a great circle course, preferring to pick a course or series of courses to take advantage of favourable winds and currents, and to avoid areas of adverse conditions such as areas of fog, ice and stormy weather.

Non-navigational charts
1. Routeing charts are published for each of the oceans. There is a separate chart for each month in the year for each ocean. These show
Winds. The directions and strengths of the winds likely to occur at a large number of positions over the chart. At each position symbols indicate the percentage of winds of varying directions and strengths to be expected.
Ice Limits. Areas of fog, with percentage incidence, sea temperatures, etc.
Main shipping routes (and distances) between a number of ports. Ocean currents, directions and

rates of flow.

These charts are not suitable for plotting the ship's position or track. They are essential for trans-ocean passages.

2. Lattice charts. These are charts overprinted with 'lattices' of lines or curves which enable the ship's position to be determined from radio signals received from certain specific navigational radio stations. The message received indicates the intersecting lines on which a ship's position lies. There are a number of systems, each requiring use of the particular lattice chart designed for that system. These are discussed in Chapter 10.

3. Radio beacon charts show all radio beacons, some linking together those operating on a common frequency. They show which radio beacons are best situated to use for position finding in a given area. These are discussed in Chapter 10.

4. Tidal stream charts and atlases. A description and instructions for use appear in Chapter 6.

5. Charts of isogonic variation. These show a number of lines each passing through all points having a given magnetic variation. Variation is fully discussed in Chapter 5.

6. Co-tidal and co-range lines charts. Tables are available which predict the times of high water and low water at a number of ports (see Chapter 8). Co-tidal and co-range lines charts enable the height of tide at positions well offshore to be calculated. These are of use where it is desired to correlate a depth found by echo-sounder with depths shown on the chart at positions some miles from a port, say in mid-Channel.

Scale of charts

The scale of a chart is the relationship of a distance on the chart to the distance it represents on the land (or sea) depicted. A large scale chart shows, say, a river a mile wide very large on the chart, while a small scale chart would show the same river very small. The scale of a chart is shown, usually near the title, as a ratio or fraction, e.g. 1 : 500,000 or $\frac{1}{500,000}$. This would indicate that on this chart, a distance of 1 inch on the chart depicts a distance of 500,000 inches, or nearly 7 miles to the inch. (As the scale of a Mercator chart varies according to the latitude of the area being measured, this ratio is shown as at a stated latitude).

When selecting a chart the scale is more easily visualized by noting how wide apart are the degrees and minutes of latitude shown in the vertical borders, bearing in mind that 1 minute is 1 nautical mile, and 1 degree is 60 miles.

There are three main scales of chart.

1. *Harbour plans*. These are drawn to the largest scale and cover a single harbour or estuary, showing the greatest detail. They are drawn on gnomonic projection, but this has no practical significance for navigation. Scales are between 2 and 10 inches (50 and 250 mm) to the mile.

2. *Coastal charts* to various scales, for example : Port approach charts covering 12 to 24 miles across. Large scale coastal charts covering about 50 M of coast.
Medium scale coastal charts covering about 100 M of coast.
Small scale coastal charts covering about 200 M of coast.

3. *Ocean charts* to a very small scale spanning to 2,000 M or more.

The yachtsman will find a harbour plan helpful for navigation in large harbours containing sandbanks, shoals, channels, (such as Poole Harbour, Chichester Harbour) but in many cases port approach charts will provide quite sufficient detail. He should have a few large scale coastal charts covering his usual sailing area, and medium scale charts covering any proposed or likely passages he may make.

The amount of detail shown on a chart naturally varies with the scale of the chart—the larger the scale the more detail. A small scale coastal chart may not show all the buoys in harbours and estuaries, and details of lighthouses (their exact characteristics and arcs of visibility and sectors (if any) may be omitted or be incomplete). For this reason, medium or large scale charts must be used when closing the land and to identify lights and objects. If no large scale chart is available for a particular piece of coast, details should be found in Admiralty List of Lights, the pilot for the area, and Reed's Nautical Almanac (for U.K. and North European waters).

Care is called for in reading the scales of latitude and longitude engraved on the vertical and horizontal margins of the chart respectively. The spacings, and the meanings of the graduations vary with the different scales used. Refer to Fig 10. On the small scale on the left, each graduation marks one minute of latitude, each five minutes being alternately with and without a bar. On the medium scale shown, each one minute is alternately 'plain' or 'bar', and there are five spaces marked within each minute. Each small graduation therefore represents 0·2 of a minute. On the large scale shown on the right, each minute has been divided into ten parts, so each small graduation represents one tenth of a minute (=0·1 M).

Always read the degrees first, (taking the lower number of the two degrees which lie on each side of the position), then the minute, noting carefully the minute numbers printed. Note also what each smallest graduation represents. A little practice is necessary.

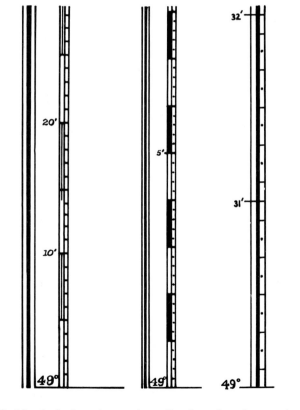

Fig 10. Latitude scales on charts. Small, medium, large scale. Each minute of latitude is one mile.

Depth of water on a chart
Coastal charts show the heights of hills near the coast, and contour lines connecting all points of a

similar height. These enable the navigator to form a picture of the high ground.

The sea area of a chart shows a vast number of figures giving the 'sounding' at each position. It also gives the heights of all prominent landmarks, hills, peaks and so on. The level of the sea is constantly changing as the tide rises and falls, so a common level is used for recording the depth of the seabed, and another (different) common level for showing the heights of land objects.

The common level used to record soundings, that is, the level of all points normally covered (or periodically covered and uncovered) by the sea is the chart datum (CD). Chart datum is the level of the sea at or near the Lowest Astronomical Tide (LAT) which is the lowest level to which the tide is expected to fall due to astronomical conditions. Normally the sea will be above that level but occasionally when affected by strong winds, storm surges or high barometric pressure, it may fall below chart datum. Depth of water below chart datum is shown on the chart in metres and decimetres, 4.6 metres is shown as 4_6 (In UK waters all charts are metric, but charts with depths in fathoms and feet and heights in feet still exist in some places). If part of the seabed is above chart datum but is completely covered at high water, its height above chart datum is shown as a figure with a line under it. This is called a drying height. A bank which dries 5 metres would be shown as 5.

For recording heights of objects of places not normally touched by the sea, the datum used is Mean High Water Springs (MHWS). This is the average level of the spring tides throughout the year. (Spring tides are explained in Chapter 8).

Depth contours are shown on most charts. Some charts show tinted areas below a stated depth. Examination will quickly show the limit. On metric charts depth contour lines are broken at intervals where the depth is inserted along the line.

Tidal Streams referred to HW at PORTSMOUTH

Hours	◇ Geographical Position			Ⓐ 50°35'5N 1 38 5W			Ⓑ 50°39'0N 1 37 4W			◇ 50°39'1N 1 30 8W		
	Directions of streams (degrees)	Rates at spring tides (knots)	Rates at neap tides (knots)									
Before High Water 6				−6	075	0.8 0.3	064	1.4 0.7	113	0.6 0.3		
5				−5	083	1.6 0.8	076	2.2 1.1	110	0.9 0.5		
4				−4	086	2.0 1.0	082	2.5 1.2	108	1.0 0.5		
3				−3	088	2.0 1.0	083	2.3 1.1	105	0.8 0.4		
2				−2	091	1.5 0.8	074	1.6 0.8	101	0.3 0.2		
1				−1	097	0.7 0.3	074	0.7 0.3	298	0.3 0.1		
High Water				0	255	0.6 0.3	268	0.9 0.5	290	0.9 0.4		
After High Water 1				+1	265	1.8 0.9	264	2.2 1.1	291	1.1 0.6		
2				+2	267	2.2 1.1	258	2.2 1.1	290	0.8 0.4		
3				+3	265	2.1 1.0	245	2.2 1.1	287	0.5 0.2		
4				+4	266	1.5 0.7	241	1.9 0.9	276	0.5 0.2		
5				+5	272	0.5 0.2	258	0.7 0.4	130	0.2 0.1		
6				+6	063	0.5 0.3	048	0.9 0.5	113	0.5 0.3		

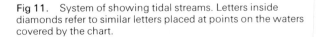

Fig 11. System of showing tidal streams. Letters inside diamonds refer to similar letters placed at points on the waters covered by the chart.

Movement of water on the chart

A current is a movement of water always (or generally) setting in one direction. This is found in non-tidal rivers, and in oceans. The Gulf Stream is an example of an ocean current. It is marked on old charts with a feathered arrow and on new charts by a wavy arrow. The rate may be shown in figures, beside the arrow.

Tidal Streams are caused by astronomical forces and change direction at just over six hourly intervals. Details of tidal streams are shown on most charts in a panel which gives the predicted direction (*towards* which it flows) and rate in knots, at spring and at neap tides, at a number of different positions on the chart. The positions are indicated by a diamond and letter (Fig 11.), the letters keying the positions to columns in the panel. The panel shows, for each letter position, the direction and rate predicted at a time when it is high water at a standard or reference port (name stated in the panel), and for each of the six hours before and after HW at that port. To use the information in the panel it is necessary to find the time of the nearest HW at the reference port (from tide tables) and to relate this to the time being considered, and also to note (from the same source) whether tides on that day are at springs or at neaps. If tides are intermediate between springs and neaps it is usually sufficient to interpolate mentally between the two rates predicted in the panel.

Navigational marks

Charts covering coastal waters and the approaches to ports and harbours contain a large number of navigational marks and buoys. They are the mariner's 'sign posts'. But just as a road sign post must be read to be of any value, so must any navigational mark be identified, and its message read.

The lighthouse is the mark usually seen at the greatest range. It tells us its name by the characteristics of its light. No two lighthouses in the same area have the same characteristics, but before using a lighthouse for establishing one's position it is essential that the light's exact characteristics are identified without any doubt. This involves counting the flashes and timing their period, if necessary over several cycles. It is best done with a stop watch. The period of a light is the time from the start of one series of flashes (or eclipses) to the start of the next cycle. Or from the finish to the finish of the next cycle. It is wise to check several complete cycles. If a characteristic is not exactly repeated, and over the same period, the checking should continue till consistent results are obtained. Never assume a light is the one expected, always check carefully. Many ships have come to grief through failure to identify a light or assuming that the one they see is the one they seek. See page 131.

On large scale charts, if a lighthouse light does not shine all round the horizon, the arcs of visibility will be shown by fine or pecked lines, and the arc or arcs will be given in the 'Pilot' or sailing directions. The arcs are given in degrees as seen from the ship (NOT from the lighthouse). (Fig 12.) They are always measured clockwise.

A medium or small-scale chart may only show abbreviated details of a light. If for example the small-scale chart states 'Fl(2)WR15 s' it indicates that over some arc or arcs the colour seen will be white and over others red. If the arcs are not shown, then it is essential to consult a large-scale chart showing the respective arcs by pecked lines. If none is available, a list of lights or nautical almanac gives the arcs of visibility of many such lighthouses. On a small-scale chart may be written
Grosnez Pt Fl(2) WR 19, 17 M but the light lists give more detail:

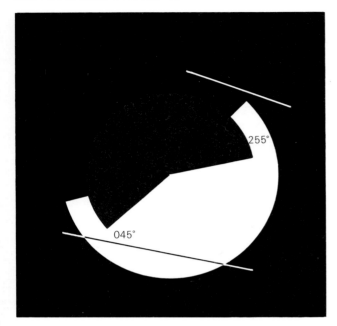

Fig 12. A light with sectors of different colours, in this case white and red. Yachts passing along the courses shown would see red, then red and white together in a narrow sector, then white. On charts and in books, sectors in degrees are given as seen from ship. In this case red might be from 255° (at right hand edge) to 45° (at bottom left edge).

Grosnez Point Lt Ho Double Fl ev 15 sec RW sectors
W 081°–188° vis: 19 M
R 188°–241° vis: 17 M
If no large-scale chart showing these sectors is available the arcs should be drawn on the chart. The simplest way is to place the Douglas protractor with its centre on the lighthouse, and oriented with the N point to *south*. Then, using the outer figures on the protractor, mark off the angles and describe arcs as in the diagram. Note that the bearings are from seaward to the lighthouse.

Some lights at entrances to rivers or harbours show coloured sectors to indicate the safe channel. When in the channel the light seen will be white; when too far to one side or the other the light seen will turn to either red or green.

A pair of lighthouses (or lights) may be placed so that when they are in line (in 'transit') they mark a safe approach. The nearer light is always the lower; the back light is the higher.

By day a lighthouse shows no lights and can only be identified by its general appearance and the neighbouring coast, its hills and silhouette. This is where the ability to 'read' the contours of the hills is of value, though one would sometimes be navigating by objects closer to the eye (i.e. beacons, buoys and the shore line).

Light vessels and light floats (which are basically unmanned light vessels) cannot, because they turn on their moorings, have sectors but have their own individual light characteristics in the same way as lighthouses. Many have a name painted in bold letters on their hull. Light vessels round Britain are painted red, but others may be black.

There is no obligation for a yacht to sail only in a channel—indeed, it is frequently prudent to proceed just outside the channel so as to be out

the mariner's map

Modern light tower is typified by the Royal Sovereign, eight miles off the Sussex coast. There is a helicopter landing platform. For the navigator it provides an unmistakable daylight identification, a light at night, RDF signal and fog horn for bad visibility.

A lighthouse first built in 1965 (Tater Du, Cornwall). It is unmanned and monitored by a local headquarters. Its automatic light runs from ordinary mains electricity but with stand-by generators. Note the multiple fog horns.

Lightships show wind and tidal stream effect from a distance as well as giving normal navigational mark information. Very gradually they are being replaced by fixed towers or large automatic navigation buoys.

of the way of large commercial vessels, but the chart should be studied to ensure there will be sufficient depth and no other dangers. (In busy waterways there are bye-laws prohibiting shoal draft vessels (such as yachts) from obstructing the passage of vessels which, because of their draft, must remain in the channels). The yachtsman still needs to be able to recognize the buoys to ensure a safe passage. But he will frequently decide to leave a port or starboard hand buoy on the 'wrong' side.

Buoyage system

Buoys and many beacons indicate their meaning, and their position in relation to channels, shoals

and dangers by their appearance, namely,
by their shape, and top mark (if any)
by their colour painted
by their light shown, colour and characteristics
by their fog signal sounded (if any)
in accordance with internationally agreed systems.

Unfortunately there is no system which is internationally agreed, but Europe now uses International Association of Lighthouse Authorities (IALA) System A. Elsewhere in the world other systems prevail: notably in North and South America where IALA System B is in force and it has the complete opposite in colours and has a further system for inland waters (the latter may be actually coastal, but dividing boundaries are defined). The appearance and structure of buoys may be quite different in the same system. Off British coasts the whole buoy, for instance, may be can shaped, but on French coasts only a top mark usually has such a shape.

There is no substitute for thoroughly learning the buoyage system in the area concerned, but basic

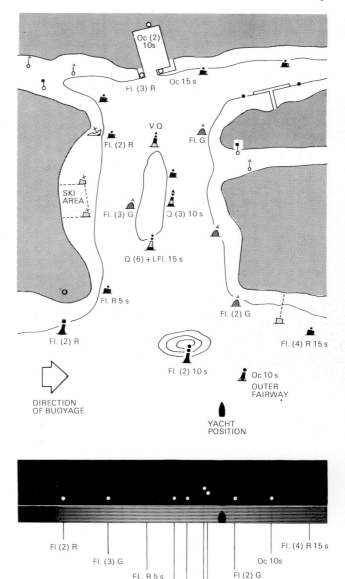

Fig 13. Typical entrance to an estuary as understood from the chart. The purpose and identification of each buoy should be known to you.

Fig 14. But approach this same harbour at night (position of yacht is on Fig 13) and you see this. Some buoys are obscured by the land. There is no indication of distance off, until bearings are taken on two or more lights: this is difficult because they are winking and can be confused. Pick three you are sure of, get a fix, use the compass and then check again as you approach. Do not rely on your sense of direction.

27

BUOYAGE

Starboard hand buoy without top mark or light. Identifiable from shape (conical) and colour (green).

Cardinal buoy south of danger painted yellow over black.

Cardinal buoy of 'system A'. Top mark is clearest item and shows that danger lies to south of buoy. This buoy is painted black over yellow. Remainder of mark is a 'mess' which is sometimes difficult to observe but includes light, radar reflector below it, bell and clapper and name set vertically across two colours which makes it difficult to read.

In European waters buoyage system A of the International Association of Lighthouse Authorities is in force. There is however always the possibility of local anomalies and 'private' methods, especially in small harbours. IALA system A is set out on pages 30 and 31.

System A combines lateral and cardinal buoyage. Lateral marks indicate the port and starboard sides of a channel, using a 'conventional direction of buoyage'. This is either a local direction for entering harbour, river or estuary from seaward or a general direction (in other areas) which is clockwise around continental land masses, given in sailing directions, and where necessary, shown on charts by a broad arrow. Around the British Isles the direction is towards NE, N or E. The cardinal buoys in the system indicate, by their characteristics, on which side of the danger they have been placed. This immediately shows the mariner which way to go to avoid the danger. They are used for drawing attention to features in a channel such as a bend, bifurcation, junction, or end of a shoal. Because they are generally lattice or pillar buoys, where colours painted on may be difficult to identify, their top marks are the most important feature. Note the logic for North (two cones pointing up) and South (two cones pointing down). East and West are less easily remembered ("W for Wineglass" may help).

Lateral buoys are coloured red (port hand) and green (starboard hand) and their lights are always similarly coloured. Other buoys which are used and are most important to recognize are:
Isolated danger marks, such as a wreck, rock or shoal patch of limited size surrounded by navigable water. Preferred channel marks are modified port or starboard lateral marks and are used at the division of a channel to indicate the preferred channel.
Safe water mark, mid-channel or landfall buoy. Special marks may indicate traffic separation lane marks, firing or practice ranges and spoil grounds.

East of danger: painted black-yellow-black.

practical yacht navigator

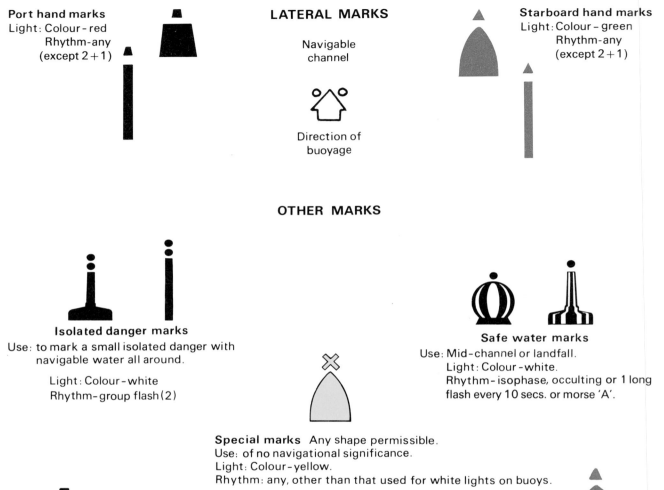

Port hand marks
Light: Colour - red
    Rhythm-any
    (except 2 + 1)

LATERAL MARKS

Navigable
channel

Direction of
buoyage

Starboard hand marks
Light: Colour - green
    Rhythm-any
    (except 2 + 1)

OTHER MARKS

Isolated danger marks
Use: to mark a small isolated danger with
    navigable water all around.

    Light: Colour - white
    Rhythm- group flash (2)

Safe water marks
Use: Mid-channel or landfall.
Light: Colour - white
Rhythm- isophase, occulting or 1 long
flash every 10 secs. or morse 'A'.

Special marks Any shape permissible.
Use: of no navigational significance.
Light: Colour - yellow.
Rhythm: any, other than that used for white lights on buoys.

Preferred Channel Marks

–to Starboard
Light: Colour red
Rhythm: Composite
    group flash
    (2 + 1)

–to Port
Light: colour green
Rhythm: Composite
    group flash
    (2 + 1)

CARDINAL MARKS

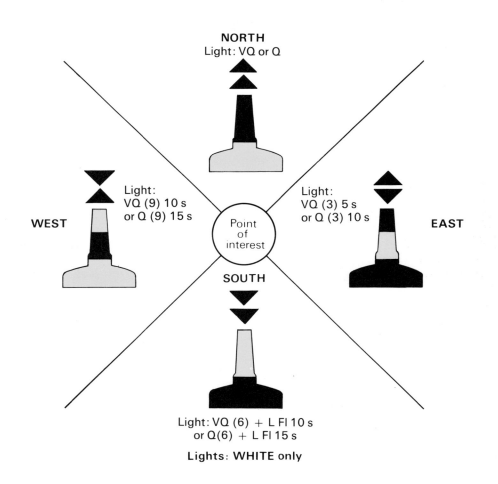

NORTH
Light: VQ or Q

Light:
VQ (9) 10 s
or Q (9) 15 s

WEST

Point
of
interest

Light:
VQ (3) 5 s
or Q (3) 10 s

EAST

SOUTH

Light: VQ (6) + L Fl 10 s
or Q(6) + L Fl 15 s

Lights: WHITE only

points to remember are (Figs 13 and 14): lateral buoys—the colour, shape or light shown indicate the side on which a vessel wishing to stay in the main channel should proceed when entering harbour, or proceeding in a clockwise direction around continental land masses. (When leaving harbour, or when proceeding anticlockwise round the land mass, the sides become reversed.)

Cardinal marks—the colour, top marks or light show the point of the compass on which the danger, such as rock or shoal, lies.

Reading the chart

The area covered by a chart is stated in the title in general terms, e.g. 'English Channel—western portion'. Before studying a chart in detail, get a broad idea of the scale of distances by studying the latitude scale.

Next, note carefully whether depths are marked in metres, fathoms or feet. This is stated clearly below the chart's title, and on some charts 'Depths in metres' is also printed in magenta colour in the margin. Check also what the various depth contour line indicate, and what tinting is used to denote shoal water of various depths. Get the 'feel' of the area by noting:

(a) The type of coastline. Are there high hills near the coast? Or cliffs, sand dunes. Are there off-lying rocks or shoals?

(b) The general depths near the shore. Is the shore steep-to (deep water close in) or shelving gradually?

(c) How much detail is shown? The smaller the scale (the more area depicted) the less detail, and vice versa. Are the full characteristics of all navigational lights given? A small scale chart may not show any characteristics of the lights of buoys, and may only give abbreviated ones of lighthouses, e.g. Fl(3) 20 M—i.e. the period of the light is omitted—is it 3 flashes every 15 seconds or every 30 seconds? As this knowledge is essential for positive identification, either a large-scale chart or a pilot book must be consulted. The full characteristics might then be found as 'Fl(3) 30s 60m 20M' (60m high, nominal visibility 20M.

(d) What tidal stream information is given (see tidal stream panel in one corner)? Note whether streams are in general fast-running or moderate. Note also the name of the standard port on which the information is based.

When transferring a position from one chart to another (as when plotting a course which extends over two charts, or when transferring from a small-scale chart to a large-scale chart after making a landfall) pick up the latitude and longitude of the position to be transferred, on both charts. Check this by relating the position to some object shown on both charts such as a particular buoy. Before starting work on a chart, rub out all old pencil markings from earlier work (hence the use of a soft pencil).

From time to time the characteristics of navigational lights (lighthouses and buoys) are changed, fresh wrecks occur or are found, and so on. These and similar alterations are promulgated in Admiralty 'Notices to Mariners', issued weekly, annually or quarterly as a Small Craft Edition. It is important that charts are periodically brought up to date ('corrected') by consulting these publications or by returning them to a chart agent at least once a year, and preferably before a passage is undertaken.

Books and tables

The following books will be found most useful, if not essential.

1. Tide tables covering the whole area likely to be sailed. Admiralty tide tables: Vol. I covers European waters; Vol. II covers the Atlantic and Indian

Oceans; Vol. III covers the Pacific Ocean and adjacent seas.

2 The Admiralty publish some 70 volumes of sailing directions, usually called 'Pilots', covering the world. These contain a mass of information on the area covered, but are compiled principally with commercial vessels in mind. Of greater value to the yachtsman are the numerous sailing directions, many written by experienced yachtsmen for areas frequented by yachts.

3. Reed's or Macmillan Nautical Almanacs.

4. The Cruising Association Handbook covers all coastal waters of Great Britain and Ireland, all North European waters and French inland waters. It supplements official publications and takes into account the needs of yachts and small vessels.

5. Admiralty list of lights and fog signals.

6. Admiralty list of radio signals.

7. Tidal Stream atlases.

Care of charts

Charts are not expensive. If well looked after, and corrected regularly, a chart should last for several seasons.

The chart in use should be kept as dry as possible and when working in wet gear remove headgear and spread a dry towel along the near-side edge. Some navigators cover the chart in use with a sheet of perspex and write in chinagraph. This certainly protects the chart, but is less accurate.

Flat zip-up cases are available in clear plastic. They are a good idea for holding a chart in the cockpit for pilotage. Indeed, two charts can be inserted, back-to-back, so that both can be read through the plastic. Some charts are available plastic laminated or printed on waterproof paper.

A yacht's stock of charts may number from a dozen or so, up to perhaps fifty. It is well worth arranging and indexing them to facilitate finding the one required. The charts should be divided into suitable groups of about six or so, possibly in the sequence in which they are likely to be required, and each chart arranged with its title and number on the near-side upper edge. Each group may be conveniently stored in a 'folio', using either a canvas, or preferably a flat, zip-up clear plastic case. List the charts in each folio, and stick the list inside, so that it can be read without opening the case. Any individual chart can then be found easily.

After use, a chart should be folded in the original creases and replaced, right way up, in its proper folio.

CHART MEANINGS *(see also Admiralty Chart 5011 Symbols and Abbreviations)*

A chart shows the following by means of special symbols and abbreviations.

1. Dangers, including rocks, rocks awash at level of chart datum, wrecks, overfalls.
2. Lights, abbreviations indicating the type of light flash(es), colour, frequency and number of flashes.
3. Buoys and beacons. Symbols and abbreviations indicating the shape, colour and lights.
4. Fog signals : abbreviations for type of sound, number of blasts.
5. Harbour features. Anchorage, berth, dock etc.
6. Buildings : to distinguish appearance.
7. Type of bottom : abbreviations for sand, mud, rock etc.
8. Topographical features : hills, contours, trees, rivers etc.
9. Coast features : cliffs, sandhills, mudflats etc.
10. Radio and Radar : stations, beacons, buoys, masts etc.

Lights. The colour of a light is its first identifying feature. All lights are white unless symbol states a colour :

R	Red	Bu	Blue
G	Green	Y	Orange
W	White (may be omitted)	Vi	Violet

A light may be shown to have one of the following 'characteristics' (see also Fig 85) :

F	Fixed—a steady uninterrupted light.
Fl	Flashing—a single flash at regular intervals.
Q	Quick flashing—a rate of 50 to 79 flashes a minute.
Fl(3)	Group flashing—a number of flashes repeated at regular intervals (in this case 3).
Q(3)	A group of quick flashes repeated at regular intervals (in this case 3).
IQ	Quick flashes interrupted by periods of darkness.
Oc	Occulting—Light being interrupted at regular intervals by a period of darkness less than the period of light.
Oc(2)	Group occulting—light interrupted by two or more periods of darkness at regular intervals.
Iso	Isophase—equal periods of light and darkness, at regular intervals.
Al WR	Continuous steady light which shows changes of colour on the same bearing at regular intervals.
Mo(P)	A light flashing the morse character shown in brackets.

Fog Signals. Many lighthouses, light vessels, light floats, and some navigational buoys give sound signals in fog (some buoys in clear weather also). A fog signal can be identified by the type of sound made and by its characteristics (number and frequency of the sound).

(Abbreviations used on charts shown in brackets).

Siren (Siren)	Medium power high or low note, or a combination of both. Uses compressed air
Whistle (Whis)	Usually on offshore buoys.
Bell (Bell)	If power-operated, a single stroke at regular intervals. If wave-actuated, irregular and may not sound in flat calm.
Diaphone (Dia)	Strong low note terminating in distinctive 'grunt'.
Reed (Reed)	A lower powered high-note horn. Compressed air.

Type of bottom. Information as to whether the bottom is sand, rock or shingle etc is chiefly of interest when about to anchor or kedge. This will give a guide to the holding one can expect. On rare occasions a position may be verified by reference to the material on the bottom, but this requires the use of a leadline and a lead 'armed' with tallow or grease to which particles will adhere. The principal abbreviations used are :

S	Sand	Sn	Shingle
M	Mud	P	Pebbles
Ml	Marl	St	Stones
Cy	Clay	Sh	Shells
Wd	Weed	Ck	Chalk

Adjectives are used to qualify some of these materials, such as

f	fine
c	coarse
so	soft
h	hard
sm	small

Fine sand would be shown as fS.

Radio and Radar. The ability to locate on the chart the positions of radio beacons and (with radar) buoys fitted with radar reflectors, and racons will enable the maximum value to be obtained from the RDF set (or radar). These are all marked on charts with their respective abbreviations.

3. Equipment to find the Way

Certain equipment and instruments are necessary for navigation, but these do not have to be costly or elaborate. I recommend starting with the minimum, only adding as more experience suggests. Let us divide the instruments into two lists—instruments for the chart table and instruments for the yacht. The former are required for 'deskwork' aboard or ashore.

Instruments for the chart table

Chart table, with adequate lighting and storage for charts.
Note books, navigator's log book.
Pencils 2B and HB, pencil sharpener and eraser.
150 mm to 200 mm Compass and dividers (6 in.– 8in.).
Straight edge or ruler 400 mm to 460 mm (15 in. to 18 in.) or parallel rule.
Douglas protractor, or other chart protractor.
Magnifying glass, preferably with in-built light.

Chart table

For use at home, I recommend a piece of plywood about 12 mm thick, about 750 mm × 600 mm, with fold-back clips or thumb tacks (drawing pins) to secure charts. This avoids spoiling a table with compass holes.

Aboard, try to arrange a chart table of adequate size, at least 750 mm × 600 mm, or larger if possible.

Again, if possible, arrange for reasonable seating— you may spend a long time at it. In suitable cases on a sailing yacht, try to arrange a strong strap which can be easily fixed, perhaps with a snap-shackle, so as to support you in your seat when the yacht is heeled over. Make suitable provision for stowage of your instruments and books, so that they will be ready to hand and will not keep sliding off the table. Good lighting is important, with provision to reduce glare back towards the helmsman. He wants all the night-vision possible, and any glare will spoil this. A fitting consisting of a small bulb on a flexible stalk is excellent. Some have a tiny shade fitted which can be adjusted to eliminate unwanted light scatter. Convenient chart storage can be provided by a shallow tray, about 75 mm deep, with the chart table forming the hinged lid.

Note Books

Without adequate note books there is a tendency to rely on memory, or to use scraps of paper. If it is worth writing down it is worth preserving to see what went wrong last time, or to refresh one's memory next time. One book specially reserved for navigational matters to enable the ship's position to be worked up at any time by dead reckoning is essential. This is the yacht's log book. Few navigators will agree on the ideal layout, but

Forward facing chart table (on Swan 37). Note ample deep stowage for gear. Instrumentation fills almost all available space on partial bulkhead.

in Chapter 13, one layout which has proved effective in practice is described in detail. Whatever layout you find most convenient to you should be used consistently. It is most unlikely you will find exactly what you want in a ready-made printed book, so if not, rule your own, with your columns and captions. Get a supply run off on a copier and put them in a filing folder. Let no one use this but yourself—anyone else is quite likely to make a mess of it.

Pencils

Always use 2B (soft) pencils on your charts. Old entries can be rubbed out, but a hard pencil is difficult to remove and permanently marks the chart—and good charts are not cheap. Buy a box of 2B pencils while you are about it. HB or H pencils can be used for log entries and other work—this should not require erasure, and a hard pencil stays sharp longer. A small pencil sharpener is a must—your 2B pencils soon blunt,

What can be achieved as a chart table on a small yacht (this is a Nicholson 30). Note athwartships bookcase, pencil and dividers rack, navigator's light and easy view of electronic equipment.

Data such as tides, code flags and deviation are pinned up for quick reference. From left to right these are log and speedometer, depth sounder, radio and DF receiver. On the chart is a Sestrel-Luard chart protractor, which enables compass courses and bearings to be read off, after setting variation and deviation into the face of the protractor.

Fore and aft chart table on *Highwayman* (38 ft 2 in. LOA) which takes full Admiralty chart. Immediate to the navigator Decca Yacht Navigator III, read outs on Hercules 190 (for log, wind speed, boat speed etc., etc.), Seafarer 700 depth sounder reading feet, metres and fathoms, barometer, bookshelf, RDF and speaker, stowage for dividers, eraser and pencil sharpener.

and you want accurate lines and figures on the chart.

Compasses and dividers

These should be not less than 150 mm to 200 mm overall, and of good quality. It is well worth getting those made of stainless steel—cheap ones soon rust aboard a yacht. Do not get the draughtsman's 'bow' compasses which are adjusted by turning a screw—they take too long to alter. Some people like the old traditional dividers, which can be worked with one hand, but the straight ones are just as good, and are more compact. Keep the pencil lead in the compasses sharp—preferably a wedge-shaped or 'chisel' point. A bit of sandpaper, or even a matchbox, is useful to fine-up the edge.

Parallel rule

This is the traditional instrument for transferring a line from one position to another on the chart, for transferring a course or bearing line to a compass rose to find its bearing or direction, for reading off or plotting the latitude and longitude, and similar tasks. There are other methods of doing these, and some navigators dislike parallel rules on the grounds that there is a risk of the rule slipping and giving a false result. However, a

Motor cruiser wheel house with chart table on starboard side.

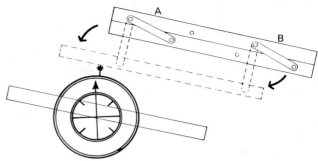

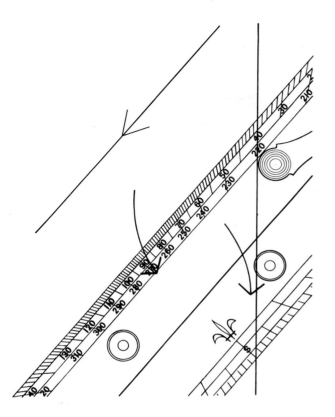

Fig 16.   Alternatively, to find true bearing of line AB, parallel rule is taken in steps to compass rose. Beware of the rule slipping.

Fig 15.   Using a parallel rule to obtain a bearing (true only). Rule has centre point on meridian, is then closed to give 220° reading of bearing on which it was first aligned.

long ruler is often wanted, and for this use alone it is worth its place.

A 'Captain Field's improved parallel rule' is an excellent type. This is engraved with degree marks along its edges, which enables the user to dispense with a protractor, or the compass rose. One edge of the parallel rule is placed along the line the bearing of which is required. The rule is then

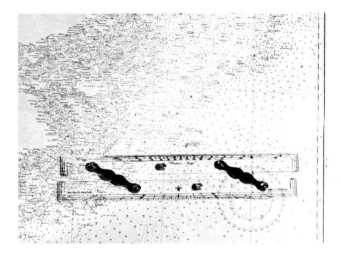

Perspex version of 'Captain Field's Improved' parallel rule. Rubber stoppers under hinge pivots help to stop rule slipping.

moved, in steps ('walked') till the zero point on one edge is exactly on any meridian (vertical graticule). The bearing is then read from the point on the other edge cut by the same meridian. The rule must be 'closed' before reading, otherwise a false reading will result. (Fig 15.)

A type of parallel rule preferred by some is the

roller rule. This is a wide straight edge fitted with a roller having non-skid knurling at each end. These make it possible to slide the rule across the chart so that it remains parallel to its original position, thus enabling lines to be transferred parallel from any position on the chart.

To obtain the bearing (or direction) of a line on the chart by reference to a compass rose, place one edge of the parallel rule accurately along the line. Holding this edge firmly, open the other 'leg' of the rule in the direction of the nearest compass rose on the chart. Move alternate 'legs', keeping the other 'leg' firmly on the chart, till one edge of the rule exactly cuts the centre of the rose. Read the bearing in degrees, from the point on the outer ring of the rose cut by the same edge of the rule. (Fig 16.)

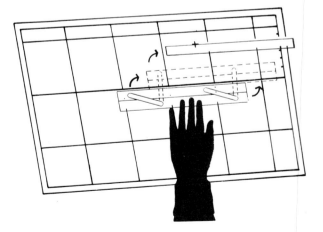

Fig 17. Finding latitude of a point by starting at a parallel of latitude and using parallel rule.

To find the latitude of a point on the chart, place one edge of the parallel rule accurately on the parallel of latitude (the horizontal lines printed across the chart) nearest to the point (Fig 17.). Move alternate 'legs' of the rule (keeping the other leg firmly on the chart) till one edge of the rule cuts both the point and the vertical latitude scale on either side of the chart. Read the exact latitude engraved on the scale. Longitude is found in a similar manner, but the parallel rule is placed vertically on the chart and first aligned on a meridian—the vertical lines on the chart. The rule is then 'stepped' across till one edge cuts the point and either the top or bottom horizontal scale on the chart. The longitude is then read off the scale.

Alternatively, latitude and longitude can be picked up more easily and more quickly by using the dividers. To find the latitude, place one divider point on the position being measured, and the other on the nearest parallel of latitude ruled on the chart and as nearly as possible immediately above or below the position. Without disturbing the dividers, now place one leg on the same parallel of latitude on the vertical scale on the chart margin, and the other leg on the scale. Read the point just found on the scale. (Fig 18.) For longitude, repeat the process using the nearest meridian (vertical line) to the position. (Fig 19.)

Dividers

If the distance being measured on the chart exceeds the full opening of the dividers (Fig 21.), pencil in a line between the two places. Then, using that part of the latitude (vertical) scale roughly parallel with the places, pick up a convenient opening of the dividers, (say, 10' = 10 nautical miles). Starting from one of the places, count the number of (say) 10' steps of the dividers it takes to (almost) reach the second point. Close

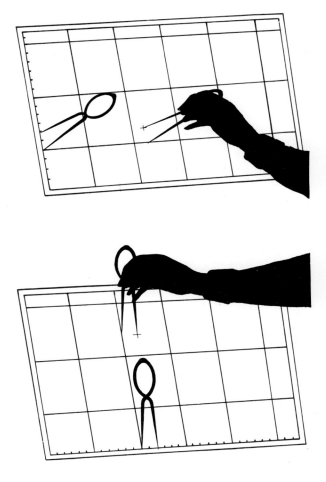

Fig 18.   Reading off latitude by using dividers and transferring to latitude scale at edge of chart.

Fig 19.   Reading longitude by same technique as latitude.

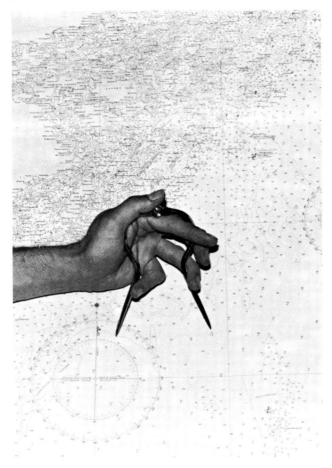

Single-handed dividers : a real aid, but not if used like this.

The correct way to use single-handed dividers.

the dividers so as to pick up this small remaining piece of the line, and by using the latitude scale again, find this remaining distance. (Fig 21.)

At 0200 on a wet, cold night the navigator is not usually at his best. Anything which will simplify his work or make it easier or quicker is then important. Here is a small tip, when laying off a course and distance on the chart from a

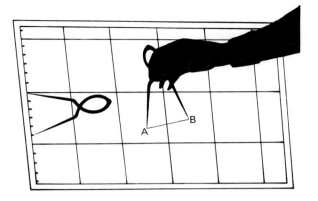

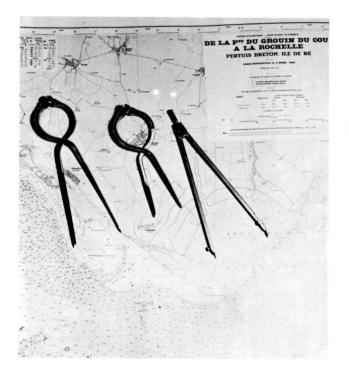

Large and small size single-handed dividers, brass with stainless steel points. Also a draughtsman's compass.

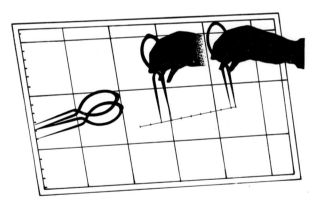

Fig 20. Simple measurement, A to B, is found on latitude scale roughly opposite place measured.

Fig 21. When distance exceeds dividers, it is measured in steps.

given position. There are two components to the job:

(a) to rule in the line representing the direction or bearing of the course, and

(b) from the first position to measure along this line the required distance.

The natural sequence is first to pencil in the line in the right direction by using the compass rose on the chart or by other means, and then to prick off along this line the required distance, with dividers or compasses, by using the latitude scale. Reverse the sequence. Using the compasses, *first* open out the compasses to the required distance by reference to the latitude scale, (using that portion of the scale roughly level with the two positions), *then* get the parallel rule (or other rule) on the required direction and cutting the first position, by the usual means, and hold the rule down firmly. Then place the compass point on the first position and describe a tiny arc to touch the edge of the rule the required distance along the rule. Finally, using the compasses as a pencil, rule in the line between the first position and the tiny arc marked.

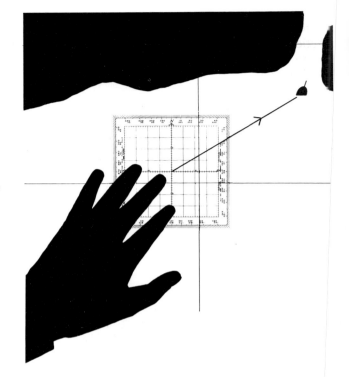

Fig 22. Simple use of protractor. Align with a parallel or meridian, put centre on bearing and read it off on outer scale (59° true).

Douglas protractor

The Douglas Protractor is made in two sizes, 127 mm or 254 mm square. The smaller 127 mm model is the more convenient for the average yacht chart table.

It consists of a square of transparent material of the Perspex type. It has a small hole exactly in the centre, and the edge is graduated in degrees all round from 0°, N to 359° clockwise (as is a compass card), each 10° being inscribed, e.g. 10°, 20°, 30°, etc. The same 10° figures are also inscribed below the others, but counting anti-clockwise from 0° N, and printed in italics. The central area of the protractor is also inscribed with horizontal and vertical lines spaced $\frac{1}{2}$ in. apart.

The protractor can be used in the conventional way for finding or plotting the true bearing or direction of a line on a chart. To obtain the bearing of a line, e.g. a course line or a line drawn between two places on the chart, the central hole is placed over the line and with its N point upwards the protractor is rotated so that any vertical line on it coincides with, or is parallel with, any (vertical) meridian on the chart, *or* so that any horizontal line on the protractor coincides with, or is parallel with, any (horizontal) parallel of latitude. The bearing of the line in question is then read directly from the edge of the protractor, using the plain (clockwise) figures inscribed. (Fig 22.)

To lay off (or draw) a line on the chart from a given position in a required direction the procedure is similar—centre of protractor placed over the given position, protractor 'squared up', N point upwards, inscribed lines parallel with meridian or parallel of latitude. The required direction in degrees (true) is found on the protractor edge (plain, clockwise figures), a mark made and the given position and the mark joined by a straight line, using a side of the protractor as a ruler (Fig 23.).

The object of the anti-clockwise degree figures (in italics) is to enable the protractor to be turned so that one edge of it lies along the line the bearing of which is required. Suppose there is a

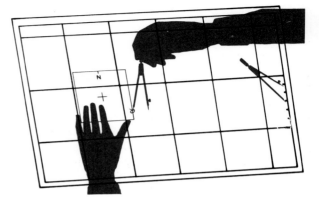

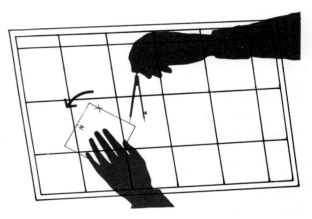

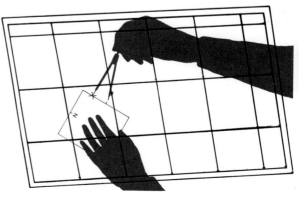

Fig 23. Use of Douglas Protractor in laying off course and bearing. Protractor is lined up with meridian and centred over starting place (small cross). Point on compass is driven in at 120° (required bearing) and required distance measured on latitude. Protractor is swung keeping point in so that same edge meets starting place. Distance is then measured along this edge or its extension.

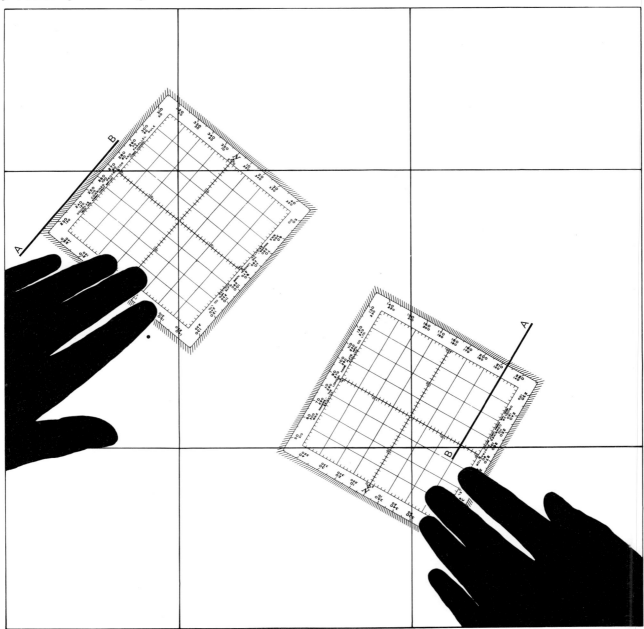

straight line drawn on the chart and it is desired to know its bearing or direction, true. Look at the protractor with its N point upwards. Along its left hand edge is engraved 'Douglas combined protractor . . .'. Place *this* edge of the protractor on the line on the chart. Now slide the protractor along the line (maintaining the same edge parallel with the line) until the central hole in the protractor is exactly cut by any meridian (vertical line) on the chart. The true bearing of the line is the reading on the protractor which is cut by the meridian passing through the central hole, but using the figures in *italics*. (Fig 24.)

If the nearest meridian is not in a convenient position, the same result is obtained by aligning the line with any engraved line on the Douglas protractor that is parallel to the 'Douglas Combined Protractor' side (Fig 25.). The Douglas protractor can also be used for transferring a line to another position on the chart where it will be exactly parallel with the first line. Later on, we shall need to transfer position lines parallel. Assume it is required to transfer PL through X. (Fig 26.). Place any edge of the protractor on X. Rotate the protractor (maintaining contact with X) until any of the engraved lines on the protractor lies parallel with PL. Draw a line along protractor edge through X. Do not worry if PL is not exactly coinciding with an engraved line: the eye can readily detect non-parallelism between two lines fairly close together. (Fig 27.). If X is too far

away from PL_1 to reach, draw a temporary line along the edge (creating a new temporary transferred PL) and work from this to X. This method is just as quick as using parallel rules, and vastly reduces the risk of slipping, as the parallel rule may do when being 'walked' across the chart. A further use for the Douglas protractor is for fixing the ship's position on the chart by horizontal sextant angles of fixed (terrestrial) objects, explained in Chapter 9.

Magnifying glass
This will be found useful for verifying small figures on the chart. A glass with an in-built torch light is handy for use at night.

Instruments for the yacht
The number of instruments to aid navigation can be as many as the depth of one's pocket allows. Some are essential for safe navigation, many are useful aids and give additional information, while others are used by keen ocean racers or fun things for cruising.
Essential are:
Steering compass
Distance meter
Depth sounder (or leadline).
Hand bearing compass

Those falling into the highly desirable category are:
Direction finding radio
Binoculars
Stopwatch

Into a slightly lower category of importance fall:
Clock
Barometer
Deck watch or good timekeeper
Sextant
Pelorus

Figs 24 and 25. To find bearing of black line on left, align Douglas Protractor on meridian: italic number (40°) gives bearing. Bearing on right runs down page. Same alignment is used, although making use of one of the parallel lines. Reading is again taken at top (210°).

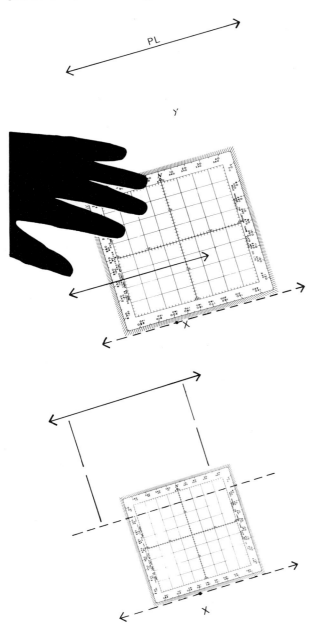

Lastly, items considered essential by the ocean racer, and nice to have but by no means essential for cruising are:
Water speed indicator
Electronic log
Apparent wind direction indicator
Apparent wind speed indicator
Efficiency indicator (Vmg)
Sailing performance computer

Compass
A good magnetic compass is an essential part of every yacht's equipment. There are many varieties but all work on the same principle. A circular card, marked on its circumference, is suspended on a pivot point in a bowl filled with water and alcohol (2 : 1). The bowl is suspended in gimbals. On the inside of the bowl a line—the lubberline—is engraved or painted. Fixed to the underside of the compass card are two or more small bar magnets, aligned on the north-south axis of the card so that the freely-suspended compass card's north-south line will always seek to lie parallel with the lines of force of the earth's magnetic field. These lines of force are 'magnetic meridians' which run between the magnetic poles.

The compass is mounted in some way so that, no matter how the vessel heels, the compass bowl (and card) will remain level. The object of the water and alcohol in the bowl is to damp down

Fig 26. It is required to transfer the position line PL through X.

Fig 27(a). Protractor is lined up with position line and new line (dotted) passes through X.

Fig 27(b). Where X and PL are out of reach of protractor the same operation is done in two steps.

oscillations caused by the ship's motion, and to reduce friction on the pivot by almost floating the card, alcohol being added as anti-freeze. A screw plug on one side of the bowl enables it to be topped up with distilled water if necessary.

Modern compasses are graduated in degrees, from north, 0°, round to 359°. As the compass must be clearly legible at some distance and sometimes in a poor light, the degree markings and figures must be well separated and bold. The number of markings and figures will depend on the size of the compass card. A typical yacht compass is marked every 5°, each 10° mark being bolder and showing the number of degrees. The last digit is omitted to permit a large figure being

shown. For example, against the 180° mark, 18 is shown; against the 20° mark, 2 is shown, and so on. Smaller compasses may be marked only every 10°, while large ones may be marked every 2° or 1°. Some compass cards also show the cardinal and intercardinal points (N, NE, E, SE, S etc). (See page 53.)

Aboard some yachts, older types of steering compass may be found with different systems of markings. The oldest of these is the points system and since a point is 11¼°, it is not convenient for navigation. Just remember that one point is something completely different from 1° and if you find a points compass on a boat which you have bought, throw it over the side. There is also a system with limited uses called quadrantal where degrees are marked from south as well as from north and this is equally confusing for use in a steering compass.

Some compasses have a transparent dome to the compass bowl, which contains a gimballed ring or 'cage' in which the compass card and its magnets are mounted, and which also has a lubberline. The bowl can then be mounted without any further provision of gimbals. The domed bowl heels with the ship, but a cage in which both the compass card and the lubberline are mounted can tilt inside the bowl to remain level at all times. This has the additional feature that the Perspex dome magnifies the card, enabling it to be read at some distance and water cannot lie on the glass. Some models have the card 'dished' which makes the far edge of the card (adjacent to the lubberline) even more easily read.

Another type, (the Sestrel-Moore) is designed for fitting at eye-level, e.g. on top of the coachroof or cabin hatch. The compass card has a turned-down circumferential edge, and one lubberline is on the after side (unlike the more usual forward

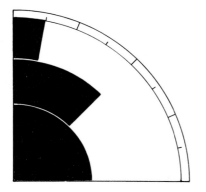

Fig 28.   Some old compasses are marked only in points notation. One point is an awkward 11¼°, but the reason is there are 8 in a 90° segment. Coloured sectors here are one point, four points and then eight points.

practical yacht navigator

side). The degree markings on the turned-down edge are slewed round 180° from those on the upper surface which are read against another lubberline on the forward side. The bowl is suspended in gimbals. The compass can be fitted with sight vanes so that compass bearings of distant objects can be taken by aligning the sight vanes on the object and reading the bearing on the flat surface of the card. Compasses are also available which can be mounted on a vertical bulkhead and again, read on the aft-facing edge (p. 56).

A Grid Steering Compass has a top glass cover plate engraved or painted with a 'grid'. This may consist of a pair of parallel lines, or an arrow. The glass can be rotated and its outer edge is graduated. The 'grid' is oriented on the north-south axis of the graduations. The compass card itself may or may not also have degree markings round it, but if not, will have a line or lines marked on its N–S axis. To steer a given course the glass cover is rotated till the required course (say 120°) is opposite a lubberline (fixed in line with the ship's head). The vessel is then steered so that the N–S line on the glass cover is over and exactly parallel with the N–S line on the compass card (Fig 29.). Some compasses can be used both as a normal compass and as a grid compass. To use such a type as a normal compass, turn the movable outer ring till the 0° mark is exactly opposite the fixed white lubberline on the forward side of the body of the bowl. The course being steered is then read on the compass card against the black (forward) lubberline marked in the bowl, the line on the glass cover being disregarded. To use as a grid compass, turn the moveable outer ring till the required course is opposite the fixed white lubberline on the bowl. Then steer to cause the arrow painted on the cover glass to lie over the 0° (N) point on the compass card. The N–S axis of the compass card should lie below, or parallel to, the shaft of the arrow on the glass.

A grid compass is most useful when steering on a set course for an appreciable length of time. It is much easier on the eye to keep two lines parallel to each other (grid line and compass card), than to keep a lubberline to a required degree-mark. This is particularly so at night. It is rather less useful if a sailing vessel is not able to hold a steady course (as when being sailed hard on the wind, as close to the wind as possible). It is then necessary to keep reading the compass course and to decide at intervals what is the average course that has been steered. For this, a

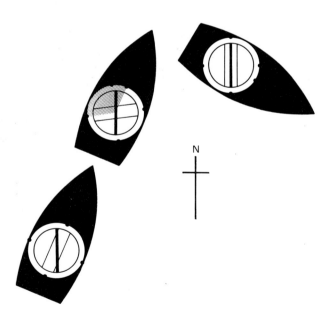

Fig 29.   Grid steering compass. From left, compass is not set, then grid frame is set to 120°. Helmsman brings grid parallel with line on card and yacht begins to head at 120°.

Flush fitted Sestrel Minor compass.

Sestrel Major compass in binnacle marked at five degree intervals. For clarity last digit is not shown: when ordered to steer 20 degrees bring '2' to lubber line. 20 on card means 200 degrees.

Grid compass in cockpit well. The type with an ordinary compass card in addition to the grid is useful when sailing to windward.

Popular on steel yachts is this Sestrel Moore compass: position above deck works aids adjustment. It can be read from above and sideways and a bearing sight can be fitted across it.

normal compass, where one reads the actual course steered against a fixed lubberline is to be preferred. A combined Grid and Steering compass, being capable of use either way, has the best of both worlds.

Remote control compasses are also available, which have certain advantages. Here, a master compass drives one or more repeaters. The advantages are that the master compass (rather

Modern bulkhead compasses are common, here also are wind direction indicators with 360 degrees and magnified scales. Logically all instruments for helmsman are duplicated port and starboard (on *Highwayman*).

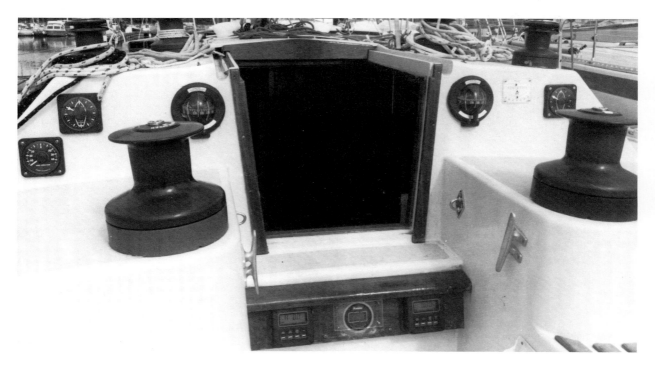

Where siting a steering compass is difficult, as in small tiller steered yachts a pair of bulkhead reading compasses is practical. Care must be taken about loose magnetic objects inside the cabin.

An electronic compass (B and G Halycon 2) which can be sited away from deviation, with repeaters anywhere and interfaced to dead reckoning computer, SATNAV or other navigation information.

bulky) can be sited anywhere in the yacht, where it will be subject to the least movement and clear of any ferrous objects which might influence it, and the repeaters can be quite small and located wherever required, in the most visible or useful position(s). Their disadvantages are that they are expensive, and they depend on a reliable (but small) electric power supply.

Compasses are also designed specifically for high speed power craft. They are specially damped to stand up to the motion of this type of vessel. These too are available with or without grid facilities.

Siting the compass needs thought. Ideally, the position should be where it is most easily seen and read by the helmsman in whatever position he may take up. It should be where parallax is least (parallax may occur when edge of compass card is seen obliquely against the lubberline). Again ideally, the compass should be sited well away from any ferrous material which could cause deviation (discussed in Chapter 5). Deviation of the compass north from the direction of magnetic north may be caused by: the engine, if within about 1·5 m, or the keel, if of iron an outboard motor, which has a powerful magnet in it a radio loudspeaker, for the same reason a camera exposure meter and any ferrous objects such as tools, iron bucket, food and fuel cans.

In this context, objects on the person have been known to upset the compass if the wearer is close to the compass, e.g. jack knife, steel buckle on belt or life harness. I once found my compass had developed an error of over 10°. After much searching it was found to be due to that most innocent and non-metallic object, a life buoy lying near it, which happened to have a wire core

in it. If the compass is mounted on the after-face of the cabin bulkhead, guard against the presence of any ferrous or magnetic object which might be close to it on the other side, inside the cabin, perhaps on a shelf. A 'Warning—Compass' notice might be put up on the cabin side of the bulkhead. Wood or G.R.P. does not shield from a magnetic influence.

Illumination of the steering compass is necessary. Some (not many) are sufficiently marked with luminous paint. If not, provision for electric (or oil) light should be made, care being taken that *any* material used near the compass is

Danforth White Corsair steering compass with guards over to prevent damage in cockpit.

non-ferrous. The light must be no more than a glimmer—just sufficient and no more—otherwise the helmsman's night vision will be impaired, and this is important. A small bulb controllable by a rheostat is ideal.

Distance measure

Distance travelled through the water is measured by three main types of instrument:

(a) A spinner towed on the end of a line in the water, commonly called the patent log.

(b) An impeller protruding from the yacht's hull.

(c) A transducer without moving parts.

For economy and reliability the Walker patent log has much to recommend it. This consists of a registering mechanism or 'head' carried on a short metal outrigger which can be slotted into either of a pair of metal plates screwed to the deck on each quarter. An eye on one end of a line, the logline, is connected to a hook in the head, which drives the mechanism. On the other end of the log-line a spinner or 'rotator' is permanently attached. This is towed through the water. The spinner revolves a set number or revolutions each mile, and the head has dials reading in miles and tenths of a mile. One or more weights are supplied which can be fixed to the logline a few feet forward of the spinner to ensure it remains properly immersed while being towed.

It is advisable not to 'stream the log' (put the spinner and logline in the water) till in a reasonable depth of water and clear of the harbour, to guard against bumping the spinner on the bottom, or getting it fouled round a buoy. For the same reason, remember to 'hand the log' (bring it aboard) before entering congested waters. If you hand the line by just hauling it in while it is still attached to the head, you will find that it comes aboard like a lot of knitting—full of twists and knots—due to the spinner keeping on twisting the

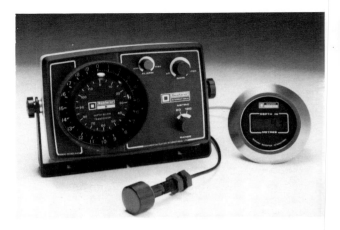

Conventional LED depth sounder and cockpit repeater.

Simple depth sounders, LED and digital, feet or metres for depths to 60 ft (or 24 metres). (Seafarer Simplex).

A digital log/speed indicator with some additional timing and distance facilities (e.g. alarms, countdowns, ETA calculation). It can take a repeater.

counter over a six-minute period; the number of 1/10ths of a mile clocked up in this time will be the speed in knots (6 min. = 1/10th hr). Or do the same over three minutes and double the answer.

Glance at the spinning logline from time to time. If it starts revolving more slowly than the yacht's speed seems to warrant, the spinner has probably gathered some weed. Haul in and clear. The counters can be returned to zero by unlatching the front glass face and turning each of the three pointers back to 0, turning them anti-clockwise.

Some instruments have no external moving parts. The Brookes and Gatehouse boatspeed sensor has no drag and is unaffected by angle of heel. Two ultrasonic transducers are sited on the centreline of the yacht, one pointing forward and one aft. Bursts of ultrasonic energy are transmitted back and forth alternately. In one direction the speed of the sound is the normal speed of sound in water plus the boat speed; in the other direction it is the speed of sound less boat speed. The time taken for the pulses to travel is measured and the difference between the two measurements is directly proportional to the speed of the boat through the water.

Impeller-type logs do not have a towed logline. They can be either mechanically or electronically operated. The 'Sumlog' is one which is mechanical. This has a short stalk protruding a couple of inches or so from the hull, well below water level. This carries an impeller which, like the spinner, rotates a set number of times per mile sailed through the water. The impeller is connected by a rotating Bowden-type cable to a counter-head which can be mounted in the cabin or on cockpit bulkhead, and which records miles and fractions.

The electronic type of log has an even smaller impeller mounted on a short stalk below water

line. Untangling it can be a tedious job. Instead, unhook the eye on the line from the head as smartly as possible and immediately start paying out back into the water the end just unhooked, while hauling in the line working towards the spinner. When the spinner is aboard the whole line should be trailing astern, and not twizzling round. It can then be brought aboard quite easily, what few turns remain being readily removed.

If you do not have a water speed indicator (discussed later), the ship's speed can be found by observing the 1/10th mile counter. Read this

level, but there is no mechanical connection and the impeller creates electrical impulses which are sensed and conveyed by wire to the log counter head where the mileage covered is displayed by digits, to two decimal places of a mile. The counter head can be mounted wherever required—usually near the chart table. With the electronic type, the impeller can be withdrawn from inside the hull for clearing, should it become fouled. Impeller type logs are less frequently fouled by weed as the impeller is usually more deeply immersed than the rotator of the patent log and can have a weed deflector built on it.

The log should be regularly read and recorded, to keep track of the ship's position, and to give early warning of a fouled log. Most logs are reasonably accurate if installed according to the maker's instructions. Accuracy should be within 5 per cent, and can be within 1 per cent. Logs tend to over-read when beating to windward, and to under-read when running with a strong wind aft.

Boat speed and depth displays. The yacht is travelling at 4½ knots. Depth of water is 14: whether metres, fathoms or feet should be known to the navigator!

Depth sounder

Rotating light meters work on an electronic impulse which is fed by co-axial cable from the instrument to the transducer, which is fixed, pointing vertically downwards. This impulse is reflected back from the sea bed, sensed by the same transducer and fed to the instrument. At the instrument the outgoing impulse causes a red light, fixed to a revolving arm, to flash, and the returning impulse causes it to flash a second time. In most instruments, light emitting diodes (LED) are used.

As the LED is revolving, the interval in time between outward and return passage of the impulse is measured by the angular distance between the two flashes. The arm is so set that the first flash occurs when the LED is passing the zero or 0 m position.

The circular scale round which the LED revolves is calibrated so that the calibration reached by the returning flash indicates the depth, at that instant, below the transducer.

Modern types may be metric or more conveniently have scales in feet, metres and fathoms. They can be switched between all three.

At feet the arm revolves at six times the speed at fathoms and at metres 3.3 times. The set may be dry cell operated or on ship's main 12 V supply (there are advantages in each). It is more economic on dry cell power to use fathoms than metres or feet. Typical current from ship's supply is 120 milliamps.

Facilities on the Seafarer 700, a popular echo sounder, includes shallow and deep water alarms, which sound at a pre-set sounding, alternative bracket or flush mount, additional digital display by liquid crystal (LCD). As a repeater is available, it is better to mount the set below, probably at the chart table. The repeater in the cockpit shows one unit at all times to save any confusion, when in shallow water.

Fig 30. A boat speed sensor with the advantages of no moving parts (the Brookes and Gatehouse sonic speed). It works by measuring ultrasonic waves' speed difference between the two sensors.

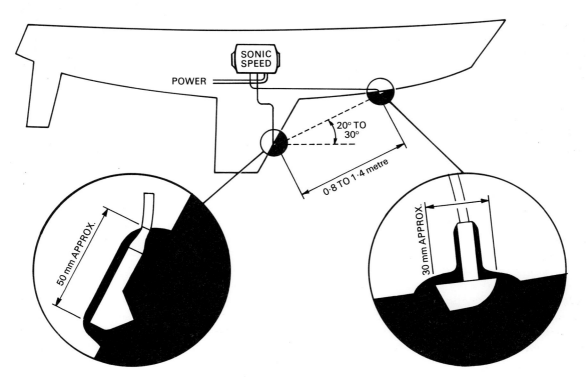

practical yacht navigator

Needle-indicating metres work on the same reflected impulse principle: they are useful as cockpit repeaters as the position of the needle provides indication without actually reading the figures, once the crew is familiar with the dial. Digital read outs are also clear, if the figures are big enough and, as mentioned, the units of measurement not in doubt.

Graphic display depth meters

These have an inked pen which indicates the depth on a slowly-moving roll of paper, similar to a barograph. By this means a continuous trace is made of the depths traversed. Mainly of value to fishermen, surveyors and the like, these are not necessary for the cruising yacht. Like all echo-sounders, this instrument will pick up shoals of fish.

The neon type or LED echo-sounder has three characteristics to commend it:

(a) Usually it is the least expensive.
(b) Easily read at night—the position of the flashes relative to the flash at the zero point indicates the depth without recourse to reading the dial; e.g. 25 ft or fathoms flash comes up at the 25 minute position on a clock face.
(c) The setting being used, feet or fathoms, is readily seen by the frequency of the flashes—almost continuous when on feet; distinct and separate flashes when set for fathoms.

The echo-sounder has now superseded the leadline because of the speed and frequency with which soundings can be taken with it, and the elimination of the hard work and skill required to use the leadline. The only points in favour of the old leadline are its simplicity and the facility it gives of determining the material on the seabed by 'arming' the lead with tallow so that particles of sand, shell or whatever is there adhere to the lead.

THE PELORUS COMPASS

A pelorus compass is used when the steering compass is so positioned that it is difficult to take bearings of a landmark direct from the steering compass. A pelorus is a dummy compass in which the compass card is moved by hand instead of by magnetic forces. It consists of a base fitted with a lubberline; a compass card on a central pivot which can be turned by hand to register any desired 'course' against the lubberline and can be locked in that position; sight vanes pivoting on the central pivot so that a distant object can be 'sighted' and its bearing read off on the dumb compass card.

To operate the pelorus, the base plate is fixed (or firmly held) so that the lubberline and central pivot are on a line exactly parallel with the fore-and-aft line of the yacht. (A convenient place may be on the top of the coachroof with the aft side of the pelorus base butted firmly against any (exactly) athwartships moulding.)

If the next bearing to be taken is that with the yacht's head 135°C, the pelorus compass card is unlocked, the card turned till 135° is opposite the lubberline, and the card re-locked. The sight vanes are then turned till they are sighted on the object while the helmsman reports he is steering on 135° by his compass. The object's bearing is then read on the pelorus card under the sight vane's pointer. As both steering compass and pelorus are reading the same heading, the bearing by pelorus will be the same as if taken with the steering compass. As the helmsman is directed to steer on a fresh course (say 180°), the pelorus dumb card is unlocked, re-aligned on 180° to its lubberline, and re-locked. When the helmsman reports he is on the new course the sight vane is directed on to the object and the pelorus bearing is taken and recorded.

This would also be the procedure when swinging ship to check for compass error, as described on page 78.

A neon-type echo sounder will give some indication of the composition of the seabed. When over rock, the indicating flash forms a sharp line : when over soft mud the impulse is blurred and the neon light is wider.

The transducer should be fitted in accordance with the makers' recommendations. In a sailing yacht consideration should be given to fitting two transducers, one on each side of the keel, so that when the yacht is heeled over steeply when sailing on a tack, the leeward transducer will be 'pointing' more or less vertically downwards. Switches are available which, working under gravity, automatically switch from windward to leeward transducer. If two are decided upon, they must be ordered as a pair as each transducer is matched.

In yachts having GRP hulls it is normal to fit transducers which are entirely inside the hull. This avoids having the hull skin broken, and there are no skin fittings, but the maximum operating depth may be slightly reduced. Special fitting is necessary to ensure the impulse and reflection are both transmitted through the hull. When fitting a transducer to a power boat—particularly a fast planing type—care must be taken to fit it in a hull position where the water will be least turbulent, as this can interfere with correct functioning.

Hand bearing compass

There are many occasions when the navigator will wish to find the compass bearing from the yacht of one or more distant objects to determine the yacht's position in relation to that object or objects, such as lighthouse, headland or church tower. Few steering compasses are positioned to enable that compass to be used for this purpose with any ease. A hand bearing compass, as the name implies, is a small, easily portable compass,

A mini handbearing compass, easily used in difficult conditions from any part of the boat. An important aid for coastal pilotage.

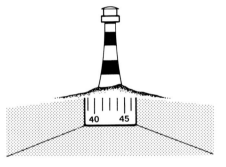

Fig 31. View through mini-handbearing compass. At night Betalight shows scale. A new Minicompass model is fitted with an additional lens mounted into the top face. This permits reading the compass bearing with the eye vertically over the compass, enabling it to be used as an emergency steering compass.

usually with a prism over one edge. The prism and associated backsight are lined up by eye with the object, (Fig 31.) and in the prism will be seen a reflection of the edge of the compass card, from which the object's bearing can be read. These compasses usually have either a self-contained torch light with battery in the handle, or glowing luminous material ('Betalight'). When not being used, the handle type compass should always be secured to a bulkhead. A handbearing compass is essential to determine whether a risk of collision exists with an approaching vessel.

4. More on Instruments

Ordinary radio broadcasts give time signals and weather forecasts (as well as entertainment and news), but the same set, if a marine one, is likely to have the radio beacon band of 285 to 315 KHz. Together with VHF and specialized receivers, the following is the range of radio navigational aids. 1. Marine radio beacons. 2. Aeronautical beacons. 3. Decca. 4. Loran C. 5. Omega. 6. Satellite navigation. 7. Radar and Racons. 8. VHF radio lighthouses. 9. VHF direction finding.

Marine and aeronautical beacons give a single position line and only require a simple combined hand antenna and compass to find a bearing. The equipment is long established, but an amount of practice is needed to obtain good results.

The ferrite rod antenna will give the minimum signal strength when aligned parallel with the direction of the transmitting station, i.e. pointing directly towards or away from the station, and the maximum when its axis is at right angles to the line to the station.

In practice it is found that the 'null' point—the position of the antenna which gives the weakest signal— is much more clearly identifiable than the position of maximum signal strength. The antenna, therefore, is rotated to find the exact position of minimum signal strength. On a good set tuned to a station well within range there will be one position where the signal will be quite silent. This is the 'null' point.

The ferrite rod antenna is mounted either above or below a small compass. The antenna-and-compass unit is connected to the radio set by a coaxial cable. The antenna together with its compass can be rotated by hand till the 'null' position is found, and the compass bearing of the antenna, and hence of the transmitting station found at once, without reference to the steering compass.

Most sets will give identical results whether the antenna is pointed AT the transmitting station, or exactly AWAY from it. Normally one has a rough idea of the general direction of the station to which the set is tuned, but ambiguity can arise in the case of an offshore station such as a light vessel. It can happen that the station is somewhere astern of the yacht when it is thought to be ahead (or vice versa). (Fig. 32b.). Some sets incorporate a device for resolving this possible ambiguity, i.e. will indicate which end of the rod is pointing to the station and which away from it.

Almost all DF radios are also capable of receiving long and medium wave transmissions, so that shipping and general weather forecasts and news can be received. When using celestial navigation frequent radio time signals are essential, and these too can be received. For good results, DF radio receivers should be so sited that the antenna is in a position least subject to radio distortion, and the compass clear of anything that may cause deviation. A DF receiver should be

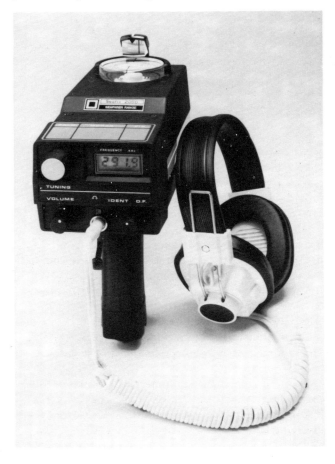

A hand held RDF (Seafix 2000) with directly read compass and digital read out for frequency. It operates on a dry battery in the handle.

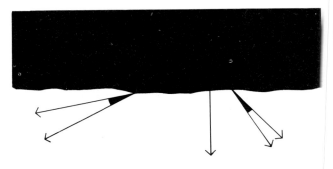

Fig 32a. When radio bearings are taken so that they pass near the coast, refraction usually occurs. The bearing which crosses the coast at right angles is not affected.

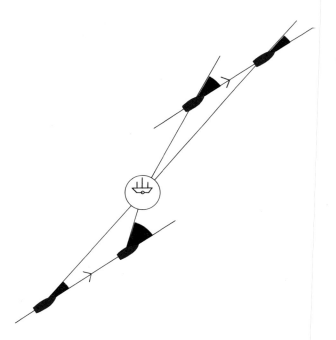

Fig 32b. Which side of the light ship am I? Radio bearing could be 180° out. For yacht on set course, change of angle gives clue. If bearing opens out, beacon is ahead of the beam; if it reduces, beacon is abaft beam.

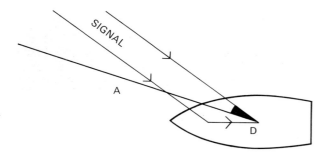

Fig 32c.   Quadrantal error. Signals from radio beacon approach yacht, but part of them are deflected (D), so that navigator interprets signal as coming from A.

'calibrated' by sailing within sight of a radio beacon (transmitting station) and taking both radio and visual bearings of the station with the ship heading successively on courses all round the compass.

Binoculars

It is surprising how often binoculars are used, to search for a buoy or lighthouse or other landmark, or even to read the name of a buoy, or of a ship. It is a mistake to buy glasses of too high a power. Magnification ×5 or ×7 is the maximum to be of practical value at sea. The higher the power the more the object viewed will 'dance'. Magnification ×10 is almost useless, even in a flat calm. The more important feature of binoculars is the size of the object lens (the larger end). The bigger they are the better will be the light-gathering power, and this determines their value when observing in a poor light or at night. The ideal size is 7 × 50 (indicating magnification of 7, diameter of object glass 50 mm), 7 × 35 is also a useful size, and has the advantage of being smaller and lighter than 7 × 50.

Stop watch

This is useful for timing lights. The light should be observed and the stop watch used to time it carefully. This is accurate and far more reassuring than trying to count.

Clock

A clock with a quartz movement on the cabin bulkhead is obviously useful. One which chimes 'ship's bells' is rather fun, and (if set a few minutes fast) can be a useful reminder of the time to tune in to the next shipping forecast, the time to read the patent log, and to change watches.

For small craft, the best way of radio direction finding is an antenna connected direct to a compass. This is a ferrite rod (Brookes and Gatehouse) which gives a minimum signal in the line of the beacon.

Watertight radio receiver for broadcasts and RDF bands. Timer incorporated to switch on as required (e.g. for weather forecasts) and for RDF timings.

Barometer

A barometer can give additional indications of changes in the weather. On a passage of 24 hours or more it is prudent to make the reading of the barometer one of the routine items to be noted in the logbook at regular intervals. Any marked change indicates a probable change in the weather, and if readings are regularly recorded a graph of the barometric pressure can easily be constructed. (Fig 33.). Alternatively, some yachts carry a barograph, a barometer which traces on paper a continuous record of the reading. Hardly necessary on a coastal cruiser, this type is of particular value when in tropical waters where a change of as little as 3 millibars may give warning of an approaching cyclone.

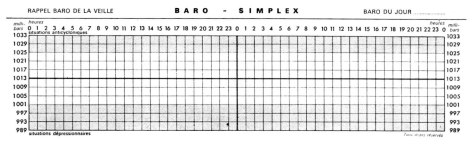

Fig 33.   If a barograph is not carried, a graph can be constructed to show the movement of the barometer. This 'Baro-Simplex' is a 24-hour chart for such use. (It is published by Editions de la Mer, Paris).

The Sextant

Essential for long-distance cruising when celestial observations are necessary, a sextant can be of value even in coastal cruising. A sextant is designed to measure with great accuracy the angle subtended at the observer between two objects. If the angle between the top of an object and the sea level below it is measured, then if the height of the object is known it is a moment's work to find out the distance from the object. The height of all lighthouses is available, for example. This is a vertical sextant angle (VSA). Similarly, the horizontal angle between two objects or features can be measured by horizontal sextant angle (HSA). The procedure for obtaining and using VSAs and HSAs is given in Chapter 9.

Even when making modest passages there may well be occasions when a position line or position found by a celestial observation of the sun (or moon, planet or star) will be of value. For this a sextant is essential.

Apparent wind direction indicator

The movements of an arrow, fixed to the masthead and free to pivot like a weathercock, wind sock or

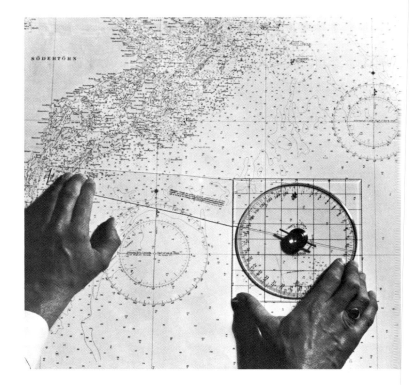

A popular alternative to parallel rules. On the Hurst
Plotter, the circular compass scale is clamped on to the square
grid to show magnetic variation. When the grid is aligned with
meridians and latitudes, the swinging arm then reads off
magnetic courses and bearings without the need to convert
(deviation where it exists, must be applied).

burgee, are transmitted electronically to a dial. A
pointer shows the direction and number of degrees
which the masthead arrow is pointing from the
dead-ahead position. Note that this will register
only the direction, relative to the ship's head, of
the apparent wind, not the true wind. The

instrument is of value in helping to steer the
optimum course when close-hauled, particularly
at night when the sails cannot readily be
observed, and also for the less experienced
helmsman. The skipper who knows his boat can
instruct the helmsman to steer a course which

keeps the apparent wind, say 32° on the port bow, if he knows this is the best angle to the wind in the prevailing conditions. The wind direction indicator is a great help when running down wind with the wind almost dead astern—particularly at night.

The wind speed indicator, or anemometer

This consists of four small hemispherical cups mounted on four arms free to rotate on a vertical axis, carried at the masthead and electronically connected to a dial which translates the revolutions of the cups into wind speed in knots. Knowledge of the wind speed in absolute terms (knots) can reinforce judgement as to when to reef, what sail to carry, and so on. For the skilled racing skipper it can also indicate the optimum close-hauled course to steer. It can also support the bar story about how it was 'blowing 50 knots'.

Integrated navigation systems

Once an owner begins to add electronics to the yacht's equipment, he will find it advantageous to relate the various readings to each other. For instance, by combining boat speed, apparent wind speed and apparent wind angle it is possible to calculate true wind speed and angle relative to the boat. This can be done by drawing a little vector diagram; but of course one does not. Instead one employs the microchip.

The latter means that ever more compact computers, with low current usage, can be installed even in small sailing yachts relying on 12-volt batteries. Now the tendency is to link more and more input in order (a) to derive additional information and (b) to incorporate such information on a limited number of displays.

The displays can be digital, analogue (pointers on dials), audible (usually alarms and alerts), coloured lights or even on a VDU (visual display unit similar to a domestic television screen).

For navigation Decca or Loran can be linked to satellite navigation and to a dead reckoning computer. The latter is not so desirable since Decca etc. can give an instant position regardless of drift, but dead reckoning is needed if SATNAV is in use and giving readings only periodically. Such basic

Stopwatch for use on deck, essential for easy timing of lights: this one is sealed in plastic.

practical yacht navigator

navigational requirements as time are available in the system as a matter of routine together with an alarm clock. This latter may not be needed for weather forecasts if a receiver which switches itself on at programmed times is on board!

Fig 34 shows the Hercules 2 system of Brookes and Gatehouse Ltd. In this and other integrated systems, the autopilot can be switched straight on and locked on to the desired course. Secondary data can be obtained with the use of sensors for heel angle, rudder angle, water temperature, fuel level and so on.

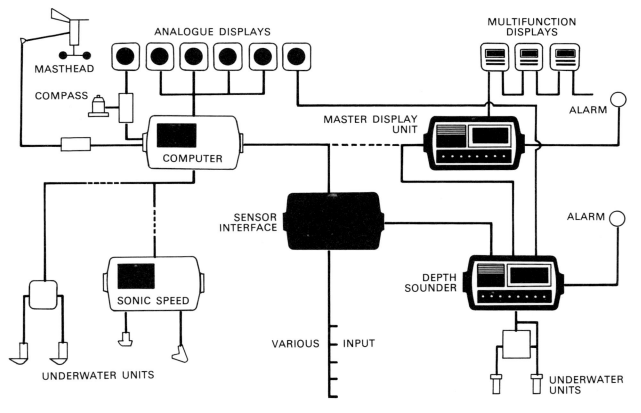

Fig 34.   An integrated navigational instruments system. The Brookes and Gatehouse Hercules 2 monitors and computes a host of data when sailing. Analogue dials and multifunction digital displays are on deck and a master display unit, which can give several digital readings simultaneously, is at the chart table below. Information from SATNAV or other position fixing systems can be interfaced, as can an autopilot for immediate auto steering of desired course.

5. North, South, East, West

Whenever we are out of sight of land and quite frequently when within sight of the coast, the only way to tell the heading is by using the compass. The compass is quite the most important instrument on the yacht, so a clear understanding of how to use it is essential.

As the lubber line shows the exact direction of the yacht's fore-and-aft line, the direction in which the yacht is pointing is given by the degree mark on the compass card which is against the lubber line. In a yacht under way and changing direction, one's first impression is that the compass card is swinging and that the lubber line is stationary. But really the compass card remains (relatively) stationary, the N point constantly pointing to north, and it is the lubber line which is moving round the compass card as the yacht's head moves round. But the north to which the card tries to point is called magnetic north. It is not the same as true north and indeed the whole card is slewed round so that every reading on it will differ from the true direction by the same amount. (Fig 35.). It follows that a magnetic direction, heading or bearing is likely to differ from the corresponding true direction or bearing read from the chart. This difference, (or 'error') is called VARIATION.

To relate a compass reading to a true bearing on the chart, the compass reading must be converted to the corresponding true bearing. In the same way any bearing picked up from the chart by reference to the meridians, which all run true north and south, must be converted to the corresponding magnetic bearing before being used for steering. This is the application of variation.

Variation
Variation may be either side of the true direction of

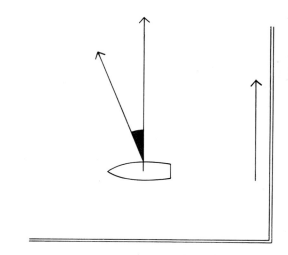

Fig 35. The yacht's compass seeks to point to magnetic north (coloured arrow). But true north is shown by the edge of the chart and every meridian and there is an angular difference. This difference is variation.

north. For instance in Western Europe the variation is between 0° west and 10° west. Near Vancouver Island in Canada the variation is as much as 24° east, while near Greenland it is 50° west, because there it is getting very close to the actual north magnetic pole.

So to relate any reading on the compass to the true bearing on the chart the compass reading must be converted to the corresponding true bearing.

Now to find what the variation is:

(a) By looking at the compass rose printed on the chart.
Sometimes it says 'variation 7° west (1987) decreasing about 6' annually'. Obviously these six minutes multiplied by years elapsed must be applied to bring it up to date for the year in which you are.
(b) Many nautical almanacs and pilots give the variations at various ports. Some ocean and other small scale charts show variation by means of isogonic lines on them.

Deviation

Steel or other magnetic material near the compass, whether loose gear or the yacht's structure itself causes deviation. When variation has been applied to a true bearing it is known as a magnetic reading: when deviation has been applied on top of this it is known as a compass bearing or course and is written 010° C or 174° C. In a wooden or GRP yacht a well sited compass may have no deviation if the engine and iron keel are far enough away. Usually on GRP yachts the deviation is extremely small and of the order of not more than 2°. Beware however of metal objects which can influence the compass if left carelessly near it. This is old advice but one sees it happen quite frequently. An ordinary so-called stainless steel

crew knife when near the compass will be seen to have a tremendous effect and can significantly deflect the compass needle. One idea is to have a notice in the cabin if the compass position is on the other side of the bulkheads, stating that the compass is there and that no metal materials must be put in that region of the cabin

Having removed all possible influences from the compass it is still necessary to see if there is any deviation remaining and this is done by 'swinging ship'. Bearings are taken with the steering compass of a distant object the magnetic bearing of which is already known or has been found. The yacht heads on each of eight or more equidistant headings all round the compass. Each bearing of the object taken with the compass is compared with the actual magnetic bearing of the object from the yacht's position, the difference being the deviation on that heading.

The reason for this becomes apparent when we consider the effect, for example, of having a single piece of metal which attracts the compass north and repels its south pole, placed, say, forward of the compass. (Fig 36.) Note the effect the metal will have on the compass needle as the yacht's head is steadied in different directions. Or take the case where a single piece of metal which attracts the compass N and repels its S pole is placed on the port quarter. (Fig 37.) This is an over-simplification of the problem, but will serve to illustrate how magnetic influences in the yacht may affect the compass in varying amounts and direction (E or W) depending on the *direction the yacht is heading* at the time the compass is read

There are three ways of dealing with the problem of deviation:

1. Site the compass sufficiently far from any ferrous or magnetic material which could cause deviation, or move the material away. There will then be no deviation.

Fig 36. A single piece of magnetic material forward of the compass deviates the card. The snag is that this is for different amounts on different points of sailing.

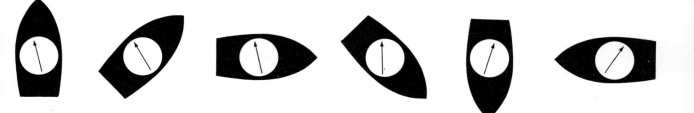

Fig 37. Metal (or magnet) on port quarter. Once again deviation changes with the yacht's heading. Note how the piece of metal moves round the compass card with change of ship's head.

2. Place small magnets near the compass in such a way that they exert an exactly equal and opposite influence to that caused by the offending material, thus cancelling out the deviation. This is what the professional compass adjuster does.

3. Ascertain what deviations occur when the yacht's head is pointing in various directions, all round the circle. In practice it is usually sufficient to determine the deviation when heading on each cardinal and intercardinal point (N, NE, E, SE, S,

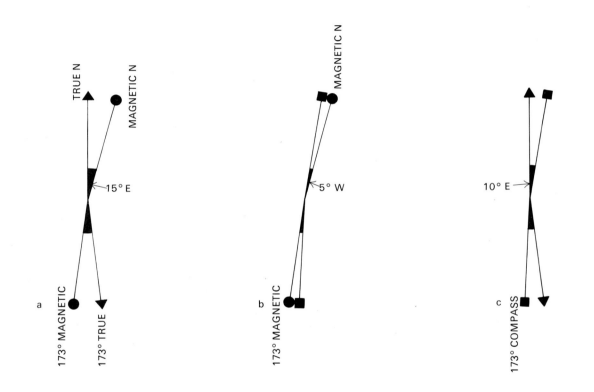

Fig 38. Variation and deviation, where present, affect every course. (a) 15° E variation shows positions for magnetic N and 173° magnetic; (b) Deviation 5° W against magnetic N and 173° magnetic; (c) Total 'error' 10° E. True: triangles. Magnetic: circles. Compass: squares.

SW, W, NW). Enter the deviations so found on a deviation card. Use the deviation card whenever converting from compass to true, or vice versa.

Compass adjusting is best carried out by a professional compass adjuster, but this is not necessary if, after carefully swinging ship, no deviation exceeding a degree is found. A procedure for swinging ship for deviations is given at the end of this chapter.

Application of variation and deviation

If deviation is present, the two errors can be combined into a single figure forming the total error of the compass: the amount and direction the compass N, (AND all compass readings) differ from the true N (AND all true readings). Each of the two errors is expressed as being either east or west. For example:

Var^n	6°W	or 8°W	or 2°W	or 3°E
Dev^n	2°W	3°E	6°E	2°E
Total Error	8°W	5°W	4°E	5°E

It will be noted that where names are the same (both E or both W) we add and leave name unchanged; where names are different, we subtract the smaller from the larger and name the answer as the larger. (Fig 38.)

Here are some examples of applying variation and deviation which are combined:

Working from true to compass:

True Co.	173°T	254°T	317°T
Var^n	6°W	8°W	2°W
Dev^n	2°W	3°E	6°E
Total Error	8°W	5°W	4°E
Compass Co.	181°C	259°C	313°C

Or, working from Compass to True:

Compass Co.	272°C	130°C	318°C
Var^n	2°E	3°E	10°W
Dev^n	3°E	4°W	6°E
Total Error	5°E	1°W	4°W
True Co.	277°T	129°T	314°T

Note particularly how the total error in both sets of examples has been applied, either by adding or subtracting, according to the jingle

> Error EAST, Compass LEAST (less than true)
> Error WEST, Compass BEST (more than true)

Having done a conversion always test with the jingle.

	Error EAST	*Error WEST*
(a)	Compass drawn to E of True N so	Compass drawn to W fo True N so
(b)	Whole compass card drawn clockwise relative to True card	Whole compass card drawn anticlockwise relative to True card
(c)	All Compass Card readings LESS than True readings so	All Compass Card readings GREATER than True readings so
(d)	All True readings GREATER than Compass readings.	All True readings LESS than Compass readings.

It would be nice if we could just call each error 'plus' or 'minus', instead of E or W. But the sign (plus or minus) to be used depends on whether we are applying the error to compass to arrive at true, or to

true to get compass. Compare (c) and (d).
This is why the jingle is so valuable, and should
always be used.

The problem of remembering whether to add or
subtract variation or deviation is a perennial one
and gives many people trouble. But really it is
similar to a problem we are all familiar with,
using a watch which is known to be fast or
slow—we have a 'watch-error'. First, remember
that variation and deviation are both 'errors of the
compass'. If small, they can be combined to give
a single figure or total error. Consider a watch
which is, say 5 minutes slow by time signal. We
know that we must add 5 minutes to watch time
to get true time. If we know the true time we
must subtract 5 minutes to get watch time. If our
watch is fast, we must reverse the signs in both
cases. Applying the same technique to the
compass, we can say that an Error WEST means
the Compass is FAST or registering HIGH; if
Error EAST the Compass is SLOW or registering
LOW.

If Error WEST:

Compass reads HIGH

SUBTRACT from COMPASS for TRUE
ADD to TRUE for COMPASS

Watch is FAST

SUBTRACT from WATCH for TRUE
ADD to TRUE time for WATCH time

If Error is EAST:

Compass reads LOW

ADD to COMPASS for TRUE
SUBTRACT from TRUE for COMPASS

Watch is SLOW

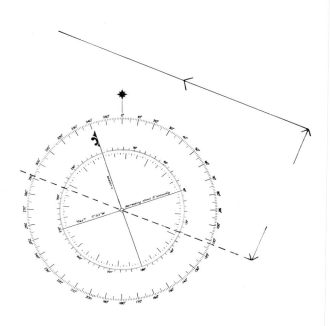

Fig 39.   The solid line is transferred to the compass rose and
dotted line shows true and magnetic bearings. True is 292°,
magnetic is 310°. (Variation of 18° west.)

ADD to WATCH for TRUE time
SUBTRACT from TRUE time for WATCH time

Mnemonic:

Error WEST, Compass BEST, HIGH, (Fast)
Error EAST, Compass LEAST, LOW, (Slow)

To swing ship for compass deviations
The following procedure can be used for
determining what, if any, deviations are present.
Two people are required: a reliable helmsman and
an observer to take the bearings. A calm day with
good visibility is chosen, so that the yacht can be

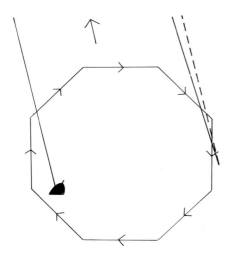

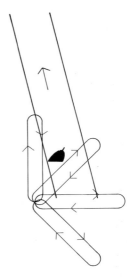

Fig 40. By going clockwise round the compass N, NE, E, SE etc the yacht strays from the mark and does not maintain the same bearing to the distant mark. By taking N, S, NE, SW etc in that order the yacht keeps close to the near mark and the bearing to the distant one changes negligibly.

held on a steady course and a distant landmark can be clearly seen.

The yacht is manoeuvred, at minimum steerage speed, near a buoy identifiable on the chart, out of the fairway, and in sight of a landmark at least 5–8 miles away, and also identifiable on the chart. The true bearing of the landmark from the buoy is found from the chart and (by applying local variation) the magnetic bearing is determined. The helmsman is ordered to steer exactly N, 0° by compass, and to call out when he is on course, AND when he is off course. The observer takes the bearing of the landmark by steering or pelorus compass while the helmsman is calling 'On—on—on'. This bearing is noted against yacht's head. This is repeated while the yacht is being steered on each cardinal and intercardinal heading. (It is preferable to take the bearings while heading in the sequence N, S, NE, SW, E, W, SE, NW. This keeps the yacht nearer to the chosen buoy and reduces parallax.) (Fig 40.) For pelorus compass see page 62.

The complete record might appear:

Bearing of landmark by chart	254°T
Variation	8°W
	262°M A

Yacht's head compass	B Landmark's bearing by compass	Deviation (A ∼ B)
N 0°	260°	2°E
NE 045°	261°	1°E
E 090°	264°	2°W
SE 135°	266°	4°W
S 180°	264°	2°W
SW 225°	262°	0°
W 270°	259°	3°E
NW 315°	256°	6°E

The data can now be re-arranged to produce a deviation card, shown below. Each deviation has been applied to yacht's head by compass to give the equivalent yacht's head magnetic.

Deviation Card.   Yacht....   Date......

Yacht's head compass	Deviation	Yacht's head magnetic
0°C	2°E	002°M
045°	1°E	046°
090°	2°W	088°
135°	4°W	131°
180°	2°W	178°
225°	0	225°
270°	3°E	273°
315°	6°E	321°

Hand bearing compass bearings
Provided the hand bearing compass is held well away from any ferrous material, including standing rigging, it is unlikely to have any deviation. In this case it will show the magnetic bearing. Bearings taken with a hand bearing compass must always be *corrected for variation* to provide a *true bearing*.

Approximate deviation check in emergency
If for any reason the deviations are not known, or are in any way suspect, for instance on taking an unknown yacht to sea without having had the compass swung, or if the deviation card is missing or lost, a rough guide to the deviation on just one course can be got by holding up a good hand bearing compass, well away from shrouds or any metal, and sighting the mast and bow while standing exactly amidships in the stern. Compare the reading obtained with that shown by the yacht's steering compass and note any difference. This will be the approximate deviation. Variation

must still be applied in the usual way. This is apt to be rough and ready but will guard against any gross error. But remember that the deviation so found is only valid for the course being steered at the time, and may be very different on a different yacht heading. This is not recommended on an all-steel yacht, for obvious reasons.

Using magnetic bearings
Some navigators prefer to work entirely with magnetic bearings, using the *inner* ring of the compass rose on the chart, and parallel rule. Alternatively, a 'Hurst', 'Sestrel Luard' or similar protractor can be used. (A 'Hurst' is shown on page 39; a 'Sestral Luard' on page 38).
To use one of these, for magnetic bearings, the rotatable transparent rose is displaced by the amount and direction of local variation, the square transparent base aligned on any convenient meridian or parallel, and the magnetic bearing of the ruler or cursor is read on the transparent rose. If the steering compass is subject to deviation, there is provision for setting this also on the protractor so that the ruler then indicates the compass course or bearing.

  Points to watch when using this type of protractor are:
(a) Use the variation given on the chart compass rose which is nearest to the position, and see that the variation given is up to date.
(b) If deviation is present, it will be necessary to re-set the protractor for the particular deviation for ship's head at the time, and to alter this on change of ship's head, if a course to steer is being sought.
(c) Bearings of leading lines, arcs of visibility etc shown on Admiralty charts are always true (without the suffix T), not magnetic. On other charts and in some pilot books they may be either

magnetic or true, so carefully note which it is. If there is no suffix it is safe to assume a bearing is true.

6. To Shape a Course

Now that we have surveyed the tools of navigation, let us see how to use them to sail from one point to another. Even if there are no obstructions, sandbanks, pieces of land and so on in the way it may not be possible to sail direct because of the necessity to tack. Before dealing with that a bit later, assume that you are under power or have a fair wind, and can steer the course required.

Even this may not be the way in which the yacht is actually going and she may be deflected by:
(a) The effect of any tidal stream (or other current) setting across the track.
(b) The effect of leeway due to wind blowing across the track, causing the yacht to drift to leeward.

First we must find out, by whatever evidence is available, what the tidal stream is doing, or will be doing, when the course is sailed. We must find both the direction the stream will be flowing (known as 'set') and the speed. Then we must estimate as best we can what leeway the yacht will be making. Only when both factors have been assessed as closely as possible can we work out the course we must steer to remain on the desired track.

Tidal stream

It is common knowledge that tides are caused by the moon and the sun, and that the whole body of a large area of the sea moves to and fro twice a day. As it moves in one direction the level of the sea rises, and as it moves away it falls. There are thus two movements, one a lateral movement, which is the tidal stream, the other vertical movement resulting in changes in the height of tide. Both concern the navigator, but for purposes of shaping a course we need only consider the lateral movement or tidal stream (except for consideration of making short cuts over shoals).

Everything that floats is affected by the stream to the same extent. The difference is that for a slower boat, it takes her longer to move a given distance through the water and therefore she is exposed to a particular tidal stream for a greater time than a fast boat.

Think of the sea as an enormous conveyor belt moving in the direction of the stream. An ant walking due north across a conveyor belt moving due east cannot tell that he is moving (relative to the shop floor) in a direction well east of north—he is moving in a diagonal direction over the floor, though straight across the conveyor belt. Similarly, the navigator, if out of sight of land or of an object fixed to the seabed (like a buoy) cannot tell what the current is doing to the water, and thus to the position of the ship relative to the seabed. (It is true that an experienced sailor can sometimes tell when the direction of the tidal

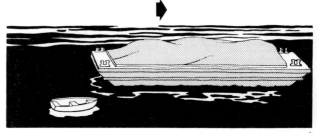

STANDARD TERMS

Certain standard terms are used by the navigator, helmsman and others when making progress through the water. *Course* is the intended heading. It is also the *course to steer*, when read on the compass.

Heading is the direction of the boat's head at a given moment.

Track is the path followed between one position and another. It may be the *water track* (through the water) or the *ground track* (over the sea bed).

Leeway (or *leeway angle*) is the angular difference between the *water track* and the *heading*.

Set is the direction of motion of the tidal stream or a current.

Drift is the total distance the tidal stream (or current) flows in a given time. (There are also other meanings of '*drift*').

Drift angle. Angular difference between *ground track* and *water track*.

Rate is the speed of the tidal stream at a given position at a certain moment.

Fig 41. Tidal stream effects are relative. Heavy sandbarge and Polycell dinghy in a three knot tide (top) lie on water, drifting at same rate. In second drawing, dinghy still adrift passes moored buoy in same tide. Next, sandbarge drifts on, but wind from the right blows the dinghy against the tide. Wind has little effect on sandbarge. Becalmed yacht at bottom moves on the tide, but with her go orange peel, plastic cups and any other floating objects.

stream has changed, by the appearance of the waves, but he cannot determine the exact direction or speed the water is moving). (Fig 41.)

Information about the tidal stream is available from several sources:

1. Most charts give details in a tidal stream information panel.
2. Some charts show arrows indicating streams and currents.
3. Tidal Stream Atlases are produced for this sole purpose.
4. Reed's Nautical Almanac and 'Pilot books' give details of currents and tidal streams.

Both the direction and rate of the tidal stream at a given place (normally) vary during the period between the time of one high water and the next, and the time of high water at any place changes progressively from one day to the next. For these reasons data on tidal streams is always related to the time of high water at a stated place. To find the direction and rate (or speed) of the stream at any required place at a given time and date first find from the tide table the time of high water on the given date, at the port on which the tidal stream predictions are based.

Note however that the direction of the stream does not necessarily change at high water or low water. The Admiralty tidal stream atlas shows, for instance, that when it is high water at Dover the tidal stream is flowing NE at over 1 knot, and does not reverse its direction until more than four hours later.

The tidal stream information given on an Admiralty chart, in the tidal stream panel was explained in Chapter 2.

A tidal stream atlas consists of a book containing thirteen chartlets of a given area. All the chartlets are identical except for the arrows showing the streams. The chartlet in the middle of the book shows by small arrows and figures the directions and rates of the streams at the time when it is HW at the stated port, for which predictions are available. The chartlets before and after this page represent the streams for each of the six hours before and after the time of HW. Figures over many of the arrows are given in pairs, e.g. 15, 26. These are the predicted rates when tides are at neaps and springs respectively. Thus, 15, 26 means that at times of neap tides the rate will be 1·5 kn and at springs 2·6 kn, and flowing in the direction shown by the arrow. Instructions for interpolating at different tides are given in the front cover of the atlas.

Most tidal stream atlases show only the direction and approximate rate of the general body of the tidal stream. In many places the tidal stream close inshore changes its direction before the main stream further out. The time varies, but may be as much as an hour earlier. This can be turned to advantage when on a costal passage by standing more inshore well before the end of a foul tide, and standing out again well before a favourable tide. In this way it may be possible to extend the period of favourable tide to perhaps seven hours or more, and to reduce the period of foul tide to five hours or less.

In practically all areas the tidal stream sets into and out of bays. Particularly when crossing a bay which could form a lee shore, due allowance should always be made when shaping a course, to guard against getting set into the bay.

Tidal stream atlases and other references predict the streams under normal meteorological conditions. Winds blowing in one direction for a considerable time (several days), and an intense depression in one area with a high pressure system in another area, can both alter the rate and the time of change of a tidal stream.

A tide rising higher (or lower) than normal will tend to increase (or reduce) the lateral flow of tidal stream. A strong wind blowing in one direction for several days will tend to push the water in the same direction and affect the heights of tides. If blowing in the same direction as the flood stream tides will tend to be higher than normal, and the time of change in direction, (from flood to ebb) may be later. The opposite applies when wind is blowing in the opposite direction to that of the flood stream.

When barometric pressures or winds are abnormal the possibility of altered rates of stream and of times of change in direction should be allowed for. Any opportunity of gauging rate and direction of the stream should be taken, by observing how any navigational buoys or light vessels are behaving, or by correlating several fixes (where these are available) with the yacht's DR positions, as ascertained by working them up by reference only to course and distance sailed through the water.

Currents

A current is defined as the horizontal movement of water due to causes other than the tide-generating forces of the moon and the sun. In coastal and inland waters currents are caused by out-flowing rivers. In oceans the temperature and barometric pressure over large areas, the effect of wind blowing (mainly) in a given direction, and the gyroscopic spin of the earth all give rise to ocean currents. These tend to flow for long periods in a set direction and at a set rate, though some vary in both direction, rate and in their exact location during the year. The Gulf Stream is a typical ocean current.

Details of ocean currents are given on ocean routeing charts and in Pilots. When on ocean or offshore passage, any current must be considered both when shaping a course and when plotting a course steered, in the same way as when in tidal waters.

Leeway

A cross-wind, that is one not blowing from dead ahead or astern, will cause a vessel to be blown sideways to some extent. Her passage through the water will thus not be in exactly the direction in which she is heading. Leeway may be defined as the angle between the direction of the ship's fore-and-aft line and the direction of her progress through the water, or her water track.

The amount of leeway, or the size in degrees of this angle, is difficult to determine with accuracy and will depend on the strength and relative direction of the wind, the state of the sea (a yacht makes more leeway in a choppy sea), and on the superstructure, sails and keel shape. Some idea of the amount of leeway being made may be got by steering a steady course and observing the angle between the yacht's wake in the water and the yacht's fore-and-aft line projected aft. A modern yacht sailing to windward may make 4° to 8° of leeway. (Fig 42.)

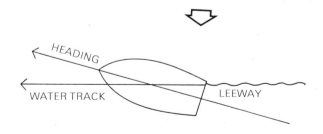

Fig 42. Yacht heads up to windward so that leeway is compensated.

practical yacht navigator

Having found the expected set (direction) and rate of the tidal stream (or current) at the time and place, and estimated the leeway, there is enough information to shape a course.

How to shape the course

Lay off on the chart the required ground track (the direction required over the sea bed), and mark this line with double arrows. (Fig 43.)

The line AD represents the distance the yacht will go *over the sea* bed in one hour, and shows her speed over the ground. The same scale is used for the tidal stream rate and ship's speed. (Use the latitude scale for all three speeds).

The water track just arrived at is still not the direction in which the ship's head must point, if any leeway is expected. We must allow for leeway by pointing the yacht's head somewhat up to windward, the amount being the leeway anticipated in the prevailing conditions.

We can now measure (by compass rose or protractor) the direction of the water track, apply leeway to windward, and we have the required direction of the yacht's head. We have allowed for tidal stream and leeway. If we had measured the water track by reference to true north, we still have to convert ship's head true to ship's head compass.

Note that it is not necessary actually to plot on the chart the 'ship's head' (shown in these examples as dotted lines, for illustration) but leeway (if any) MUST be allowed for in calculating the course to steer. Note also that (if all our figures are right) the yacht's actual progress over the sea bed (and hence on the chart) will be along the ground track and not along the water track. The latter has been drawn simply to find the required *direction* of the yacht's water track. We have only drawn a 'vector' to find the heading

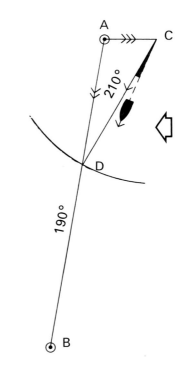

Fig 43. Desired ground track from A to B has been drawn in. AC represents strength and direction of stream. (Three arrows.) Estimate the speed of the yacht through the water. With compasses set to a radius of units of expected yacht's speed through the water (use same units as used for tidal stream AC), and centre at C, describe an arc to cut AB: this gives D. The line C to D is water track required. Subsequently leeway is allowed for: broad arrow is wind direction. Note that yacht never actually goes near C.

necessary to counteract the effect of the tidal stream or current.

Let us consider the situation where the tidal stream is not setting across the track but parallel to it: flowing either directly towards, or away from, the destination. We follow exactly the same procedure but in this case water and ground tracks will be on the same straight line, but not of the same lengths. (Fig 44.)

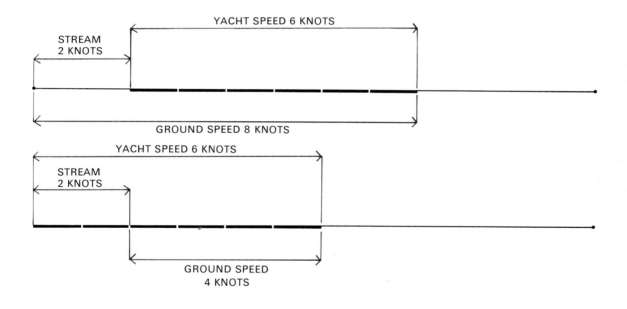

Fig 44.   Simple tidal stream or current effects, when yacht is sailing with (top) or against (bottom) the stream. It takes twice as long, in this case, when the stream is foul.

practical yacht navigator

The passage for which the course-to-steer is required may well extend over several hours. If the track will pass near any dangers it may be necessary to set such courses as will keep the yacht on the ground track, allowing for changing streams during the passage. This could be the case when passing rocks, shoals, or any other hazards. It will then be necessary to plot a series of tidal stream vectors, one for each tidal effect. For example, assume the stream is predicted to set:

In first hour   —090° at 2.5 kn
In second hour—110° at 2.0 kn
In third hour   —180° at 1.0 kn

Yacht's speed (through water) 5 kn.
Ground track 200°T

In this example (Fig 45(a)) the yacht will move over the seabed (and over the chart) along, or very close to the ground track, 200°T.

If the track lies in open waters, passing no dangers, a single course to allow for two or more hour's streams can be worked out (Fig 45(b)) From starting point A lay off each tidal stream successively from the end of the previous line. Then strike the arc of a circle from the end of the last tidal stream line, radius equal to the distance through the water the vessel will cover in the number of hour's tide used (boat speed × hours). In example (b) the same three tidal stream predictions have been used, as used in example (a) but a single water track produced. At the end of the third hour the vessel will be on the ground track line and will have made good a little more distance along the track, than in example (a). (In fact, about $\frac{1}{4}$ mile more, or $\frac{1}{2}$ per cent). A single course-to-steer will have been used, BUT her track will be in a curve, as shown. This method saves calculating several different ship's headings, and saves alterations to course, but should ONLY be used in open waters.

When making a passage expected to take about 12 hours some navigators work on the assumption that, as they will be subjected to (about) two tides (an ebb and a flood) the two will cancel out, so they disregard tidal stream. This is not recommended because :

(a) Tidal stream seldom 'cancels out' in both direction and rate.
(b) Yacht's speed may vary considerably during the passage, thus the yacht may be exposed to one stream for longer, and to another for a shorter time, thus affecting the average.

In practice it is usually sufficient to lay off courses designed to put the yacht back on the track every two or three hours, if moderate tidal streams across the track are predicted.

Other causes of drift

In addition to leeway as already described, there are two other factors which may cause a yacht's water track to differ from the direction of the ship's head. One is the effect of surface drift. A wind blowing in one direction for a number of hours causes the surface of the water to move in roughly the same direction, that is, a surface drift is set up. While this has little effect on deep draught vessels, it will affect the yacht which has a shallow draught. The amount of this surface drift seldom exceeds 2 knots, but on a 12 hour passage this would mean the yacht was a very long way off course.

The other factor may be termed luffing error. In a seaway, particularly if the waves are large, when sailing with the wind ahead of abeam there is a tendency for the helmsman to head up into a wave and to bear away between waves. Indeed, this may well be essential for comfort or safety. The course may thus become a series of zig-zags. For example, with wind and waves on the starboard bow a course-to-steer of say 240° may involve luffing up to perhaps 250° as a steep

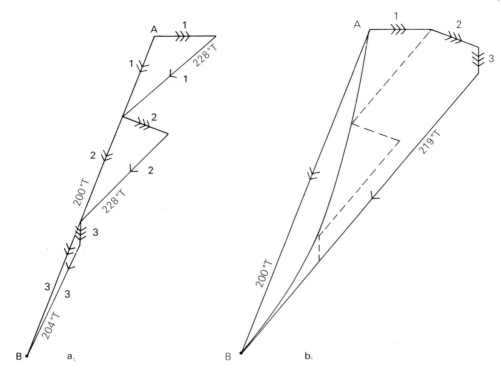

Fig 45(a). Making allowance for set of tide for hours 1, 2 and 3. Yacht in this way remains close to her track AB. Courses steered—single arrow, track—double arrow, stream—treble arrow.

Fig 45(b). Same effect as (a) with single compensation for three hours of stream. Coloured line is track over ground, not actually drawn on chart and shows the approximate track yacht will follow, sailing a single course to reach B.

wave is met, followed by bearing away to 235°
in the troughs. The helmsman has to declare (or
record) the *average* course he has been steering.
However carefully this is done, there is a tendency
for the periods when the heading is 'high' (to
windward) of the 'average' course to exceed the
periods when it is 'low' of the 'average' course.

As well as deliberate luffing-up to wave crests,
most sailing yachts when being sailed to windward
tend to run up slightly into the wind in strong
gusts. The expert helmsman allows for this when
assessing his 'average' course steered, but again,
there is a tendency for the luffs up-wind to
produce a course more to windward than that
recorded. In displacement power cruisers the same
tendency to steer up into waves from ahead can
cause the water track to be more to windward than
expected.

There is thus something of a 'push-and-pull'
between leeway, the lateral push on the yacht by
the wind, surface drift, a surface current to
leeward and luffing error.

HOW TO SHAPE A COURSE

1. Lay off ground track line from start point to
   finishing point.
2. From start point lay off tidal stream direction with
   length units equal to rate in knots.
3. With a centre at the end of this tidal stream line,
   describe an arc of radius equal to the yacht's
   speed through the water to cut the ground track.
4. The line from the end of the tidal stream line to
   where the arc cuts the ground track is the
   required water track. Measure the true direction
   of it.
5. To water track direction, true , apply leeway to
   windward. This is the course, true.
6. Apply variation (from the chart) and deviation
   (from the deviation card). This gives the course
   to steer by compass.

The first two cause the water track to be something to leeward (downwind) of the yacht's heading ; the last one to cause it to be to windward. If the helmsman is alert to the principle involved in 'luffing error' this should be comparatively minor, and the only guidance that can be given is to make an allowance for leeway, but not to overdo it. It is likely to be less, rather than more, than the measurable angle between water track and the heading direction.

7. Plotting the Course

However carefully a course has been shaped it is still necessary to keep track of the yacht's position and progress. Many factors may cause the yacht's track over the ground (and hence over the chart) to vary from that intended. These factors can be any or all of the following:

1. Yacht's actual speed through the water may be greater or less than that predicted when the course was shaped, due to wind or sea conditions.
2. Actual leeway suffered may differ from that predicted.
3. Yacht may be in a given tidal stream area at a time different from that predicted when the course was shaped.
4. Helmsman may not have steered exactly the course set originally.
5. The course shaped may have to be departed from in order to sail round a major obstruction (such as a fishing fleet), and in a yacht under sail, the wind may be such that the course desired cannot be sailed and she is sailed on one or more tacks, or gybes.

For these reasons, the navigator must be in a position to plot on the chart his best estimate of the yacht's position at any time. On this will depend his ability to make a good landfall, and in some cases to avoid running into danger. The yacht's position may be established in a number of ways. When within sight of land having identifiable features, observations of lighthouses and landmarks of various kinds can be used; when out of sight of land, observations of heavenly bodies may be obtained. Both facilities will provide a 'fix'.

Between pieces of land there will be periods—often lengthy—during which no observations for a fix are possible. Even on a coastal passage the land, or identifiable landmarks, may be invisible due to darkness, fog, mist or heavy rain. It is therefore the navigator's duty to plot on the chart the yacht's track, using all the data at his disposal. This is loosely called 'plotting the course by dead reckoning'. Plotting the course commences with the maintenance of an accurate record of times, distances and courses steered. The importance of such a record is great and Chapter 13 deals with this subject.

The procedure for plotting the course is as follows:

When the yacht is at a known point of departure (e.g. '$\frac{1}{2}$ mile S of X harbour entrance') the time, log reading and compass course being steered are all noted. At regular intervals (say every hour) and on every alteration of course the time, log reading and new course being steered are noted. If the regular log reading is missed at, say 0600 and it is read at 0615, the actual time when read (0615) should be recorded. At suitable intervals the navigator uses this data to

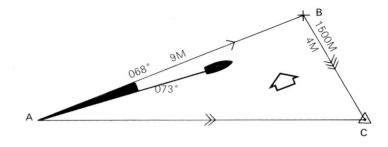

Fig 46. Yacht steers red course, but leeway (red angle) gives water track (single arrow). DR (small cross) is deduced. Add tidal stream to this (treble arrow) to give EP (small triangle). Resultant track is double arrowed.

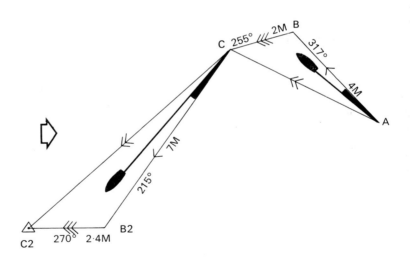

Fig 47. Estimated position after different courses, different tidal streams and effect of leeway first to starboard then to port. See Fig 46 for meanings of each line.

93

plot the yacht's position on the chart.

Strictly, the new position found by using the course steered (compass, converted to true) and the distance sailed through the water by log since the last position was plotted is the position by dead reckoning, abbreviated to DR position. (Fig 46.) But we have already seen that the yacht's actual position will also be affected by any tidal stream (or current) she may be in, and by leeway, if any. The navigator must therefore take these into account also, and the position so found is called the estimated position (or EP). This is the best possible estimate of the yacht's actual position, using all the data available. This position is usually marked on the chart with a small triangle, and the time and mileage noted against it for reference.

Having plotted the first EP, after a given time (say two hours or so) the course is plotted forward from the first EP to a fresh EP, using the course or courses steered, the distance sailed by log, the estimated leeway and the various tidal streams estimated to have been experienced.

Here is an example (Fig 46.):

From a position A a yacht sails for 2 hours on a course by compass, 085°C. On this heading the deviation is 3°W, local variation is 9°W, and the leeway from a S wind is estimated to be 5°. The log shows she has sailed 9 miles through the water, the tidal stream atlas shows she has been in a stream setting 150° at 2 knots.

First find the water track, True:

Ship's head	085° C
Dev: 3° W	
Var: 9° W	
error	12° W
(Ship's head)	073° T
Leeway	*—5°
Water Track	068° T

* Leeway is subtracted here because on this course the wind is on her starboard side, pushing the water track to the left (or anticlockwise) from the direction of the ship's head, 073° T.

The water track can now be plotted, direction 068° T from the starting point A. The length of this line will be the distance sailed through the water, as shown by log (9 miles). This gives the DR position.

Next, the 'drift' of the tidal stream in the time she was sailing is plotted on from the DR. 2 hrs at 2 kn = 4 M. The end of this line is the EP.

When a yacht is beating to windward, she will sail on alternate tacks, heading up into the wind as much as possible. Fig 47 is an example of this.

From a position A, a yacht sails on port tack (wind on her port side) steering a course 320° C for one hour when, by log, she has sailed 4 miles. The stream is setting 255° T at 2 knots, and leeway is estimated at 6°.

She then tacks on to starboard tack and heads 225° C, the stream is now setting 270° T at 1.6 kn.

Deviation on heading 320° C is 1° W, and on 225° C is 4° E.

Variation is 8° W.

Find the yacht's position when she has sailed 7 miles in 1½ hours on the second tack.

			1st tack		2nd tack
Ship's head			320° C		225° C
Dev:	1° W			4° E	
Var:	8° W			8° W	
			9° W		4° W
Ship's head			311° T		221° T
leeway			+6°		—6°
Water Track			317° T		215° T

Note that leeway is reversed on the second tack as wind is on the opposite side.

She will be at EP, C, having sailed (over the ground) from A to C to C2 along the track, provided the courses steered, leeway and tidal streams were as recorded.

Note particularly the sequence used:

When plotting a course steered, plot water track (true) first, then current. (Refer back to Chapter 6.)

There will inevitably be occasions when the data used for working up the EP are not in fact those actually applying. The helmsman may not have accurately steered the course recorded, the amount of leeway experienced may have been different, or the tidal stream may have been setting in a different direction or speed from that predicted. If any of these errors occur, the ship's true position will not be at the EP plotted.

For this reason, every opportunity should be taken to fix the yacht's true position by any means available. Whenever a reliable fix is obtained, the position so found should be marked on the chart and in the logbook with time, date and log reading. The next EP will then be worked up from the last reliable fix obtained: the previous EP being discarded. A fix should be marked on the chart with a small circle.

PLOTTING A COURSE
1. Convert the compass course to true (by applying deviation and variation).
2. Apply leeway to the leeward side of the course. This gives water track.
3. Lay off this water track on the chart and along it plot the distance from log or distance meter.
4. From this point on the end of the water track lay off the tidal stream in direction and in distance. This gives the EP.
5. A line from the starting point to this EP is the ground track and the distance along it is also the actual distance made good.
6. The distance made good divided by the elapsed time gives the speed made good over the ground.

8. How High is the Tide?

It is common knowledge that in tidal waters the sea level rises and falls between low water and high water. The echo sounder will give the actual depth of water where we are, at the moment we are there. But, what is often required is the depth at a later time or at some other place.

In examining charts it was explained that the chart shows soundings at a great number of positions in the sea, and drying heights of areas which are periodically covered and uncovered by the sea. But these soundings very seldom correspond with the actual depth of water there will be at the various positions at any given time. They will only correspond when the sea level happens to be at chart datum. At all other times the actual depth of water at a given place and time will be:

>   Charted depth—depth of sea bed below chart datum
> plus height of tide—height of sea above chart datum.

To relate an actual depth of water (as shown by echo sounder) to a charted depth it is necessary to establish what is the height of tide at the time and in the locality. Thus the height of tide is the essential link between charted depths and actual depths of water. (Fig 48.)

We therefore need precise information about the state of the tide, that is, height of tide, to be able to answer many questions which frequently arise, for example:

(a) To find the actual depth of water to be expected at a particular position on the chart, at a given time. This could be necessary when approaching a shoal or a bar across a river, or when selecting an anchorage.

(b) To compare the depth of water found by echo sounder with soundings shown on the chart, as when checking, or seeking to establish, the yacht's position on the chart by reference to charted soundings, or when taking a line of soundings. (See Chapter 9).

(c) To find at what time the water will reach a given depth at a position the sounding of which is shown on the chart, as when deciding when it will be safe to sail over a bar or sandbank.

Tide tables are available which give the times and heights of high water and low water for every day of the year at a large number of ports. But to find the height of tide at times intermediate between the time of HW and LW requires some calculation.

Echo sounder readings
A point to bear in mind is that the echo sounder registers the depth of water between the transducer (the hull fitting which transmits and

receives the impulses) and the seabed, NOT from water level to seabed (unless the echo sounder has been specially calibrated). The transducer has to be positioned so that it is well below the waterline, but above the lowest point of the hull.

The easiest approach to this problem is to measure the vertical distance between the yacht's normal waterline and the transducer on the hull. Make a note of this and add it to all echo sounder readings to give the true depth of water. (Fig 49.) These readings, and any calculations of depth, can be directly related to yacht's draft.

Causes of tidal streams and tides

Tides are caused by the gravitational attraction of the moon, and to a lesser extent of the sun, on the earth. The moon's influence is the greater because of its comparative nearness to the earth. These attractions can be resolved into two components, one acting vertically on the earth's surface, the other horizontally. The horizontal component, acting parallel to the earth's surface is by far the greater and causes the sea to be drawn towards moon and sun on one side of the earth, and away on the other.

The earth revolves on its axis once every 24 hours but the moon is moving round the earth in the same direction. In consequence the moon crosses every meridian, on average, once in 24 hours 50 minutes. The moon's attraction causes the oceans to be drawn towards areas on the sides of the earth nearest to and furthest from the moon, and away from the areas in between. At any one place there is, in consequence, a high tide followed by a low tide, twice every 24 hours 50 minutes (on average).

The sun exerts a similar but lesser attraction. At times of full and new moon the sun is pulling in concert with the moon—roughly parallel. The movement of water is then at its greatest, tidal streams are at a maximum and high water is higher than average and low water lower than average. This is the period of spring tides. At first and last quarters the sun's pull is at right angles to that of the moon, thus greatly reducing the effect of the moon. The movement of water is then at its least, tidal streams are weaker than average, high tide is less high and low tide less low than average. This is the period of neap tides. (Fig 50.)

From new moon through first quarter, full, last quarter to new moon takes approximately $29\frac{1}{2}$ days. Twice a lunar month the pulls of moon and sun are at a maximum, and twice at a minimum. Thus spring tides and neap tides follow each other at intervals of just over a week.

Tidal patterns

The pattern in which tidal levels change varies in different major areas of the world due to the shapes of land masses, differences in latitude and similar causes. The principal tidal patterns can be classified between:

(a) *Semi-diurnal tides*. These are the sort that occur around western Europe. There are two complete cycles each lunar day of approximately 24 hours 50 minutes, that is two high tides and two low tides. A typical pattern is shown in Fig 51.

(b) *Diurnal tides*. These are found chiefly in tropical latitudes where the rise and fall is generally not great. There is only one complete cycle per lunar day, one high and one low water. (Fig 52.)

(c) *Mixed, mainly diurnal tides*. (Fig 53.) There are two complete cycles per lunar day, but the

a.

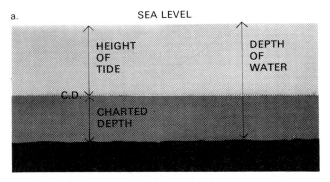

b.

Fig 49. This yacht draws 1.5 metres. Total depth of water is 3.5 metres and is detected by leadsman. Depth under keel is therefore 2 metres, but transducer depth depends on its hull position. Usually it can be adjusted to show either total depth or depth under keel.

Fig 48. A depth of water is the addition of chart depth (red tone in a.) and height of tide (lighter tone). Where the land dries at low water, b., the depth of water is height of tide less drying height.

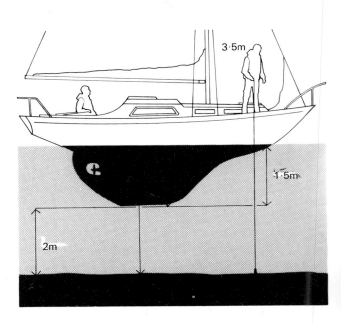

HW

LW

HW
LW

Fig 50. Top: Spring tides. Bottom: Neap tides. Each occurs twice a month.

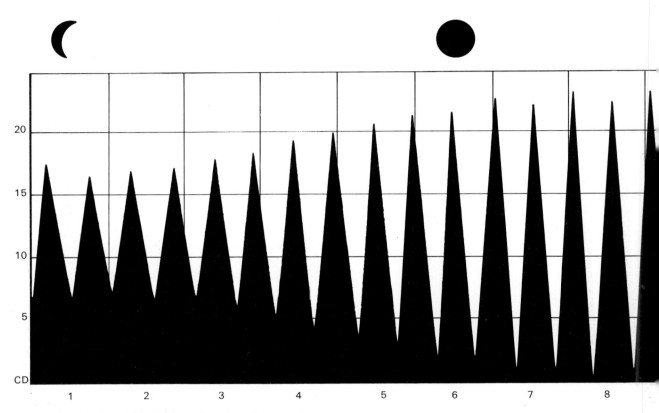

Fig 51.   A semi-diurnal tide. Horizontal numbers are successive days; vertical height in feet.

inequalities in the heights of successive high and low waters, and in the corresponding time intervals are very marked. These occur on the western seaboard of U.S.A. and Canada.

Tidal predictions

Tide Tables are available from which the state of the tide can be determined at any time in the particular year, at a large number of places. They give a calendar for each port dealt with, showing for each day the times and heights of the two high waters and two low waters. Tide tables available are:

(a) Admiralty tide tables. These are published in three volumes which together cover the world.
(b) Reed's Nautical Almanac contains Tide Tables covering British Isles and northern Europe.
(c) Other nations' hydrographic departments publish tide tables for their own coasts.
(d) Many ports publish a tide table for their locality.

It will be noted that all tide tables only give times and heights of HW and low water. Some calculation is therefore necessary to determine the state of the tide at times other than at HW, that is, at intermediate times. Before explaining these it is necessary to have a clear understanding of the terms used in describing tides. Most of the difficulty in working out tide problems arises from lack of appreciation of the meaning of the terms. (Figs 54, 55, 56.)

Height of tide. The vertical distance between the level of the water at any given time, and the level of chart datum. It must not be confused with the actual depth of water (the vertical distance between the level of water and the sea bed at any given time).

Range of tide. The difference between the level of high water and the level of the preceding or

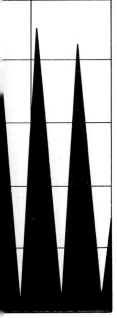

10

succeeding low water on a particular day. The level 'ranges' up and down between LW and HW. The range varies, being at a maximum at times of spring tides and at a minimum at neap tides.

Duration. The period of time between the time of low water and high water. The time one 'range' lasts.

Interval. The interval between any given time and the time of high water nearest to that time. An Interval may be a number of hours and minutes BEFORE or AFTER HW.

Tide tables

A tide table gives, for every day of a particular year, predictions of the time and height (above CD) of high water and low water at a number of ports referred to as standard ports. It also gives tidal information for a much greater number of ports or places. To save tabulating predictions for each of these for every day of the year, the table lists these secondary ports, as they are called. It refers each to a particular standard port and gives the differences in both times and heights of high water and low water between any given secondary port and the standard port to which it is referred.

The time and height of high and low water at a secondary port is readily obtained by applying its differences to the times and heights on a given day at the standard port on which it is based.

In general, secondary ports' differences are based on a standard port in the vicinity, but this is not always the case. The criterion is the similarity of the pattern of the rise and fall of the tide at standard and secondary port. (In the Pacific, many secondary ports are hundreds, and in some cases, thousands of miles from their standard port.)

Methods of determining the state of the tide at times intermediate between HW and LW vary

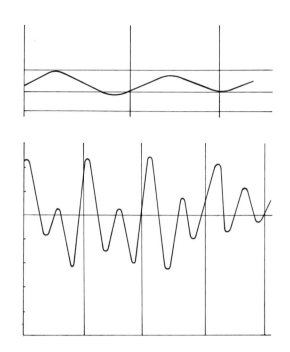

Fig 52. Diurnal tide pattern. Vertical lines are at 24 hour intervals.

Fig 53. Mixed semi-diurnal tide pattern. Vertical lines are at 24 hour intervals (example from Vancouver, west coast of Canada).

according to the table used. Three points are worth mentioning before examining methods in detail:

1. Ensure the tide table used is that for the current year. No two years' tables are identical.
2. Check carefully what time is being observed in the table used, e.g. GMT, BST, a Zone time?
3. Find the port required in the index—it saves time.

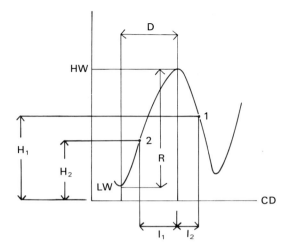

Fig 54. Terms used in tide cycle. HW and LW are high water and low water for that tide. H1 is height at time 1, H2 is height at time 2. D is duration of rise of tide, R is range of tide, CD is chart datum. I₁ is interval that 2 is before high water, I₂ is interval that 1 is afterwards. Check text for full meaning of these common terms.

Admiralty tide tables

Before discussing the use of these Tables it is worth noting their contents. Referring to Vol. 1 (European waters) the introduction merits study. Amongst other things, it explains why heights of tides may, in practice, depart from predictions due to abnormal conditions such as storm surges, high or low barometric pressures and other causes.

Part I of the tables lists the daily predictions of both high and low water times and heights, in metres, at every standard port. Part II lists a vastly greater number of secondary ports, giving for each the difference in both time and height in metres between the secondary port and the standard port on which each is based. The secondary ports are listed by number in sections, each being headed by the appropriate standard port. The columns in the table are headed:
Time differences
Height differences (in metres).

Each of these columns is subdivided between:
Times at high water and at low water
Heights when tides are

HW springs and neaps $\begin{cases} \text{MHWS} \\ \text{MHWN} \end{cases}$

LW springs and neaps $\begin{cases} \text{MLWS} \\ \text{MLWN} \end{cases}$

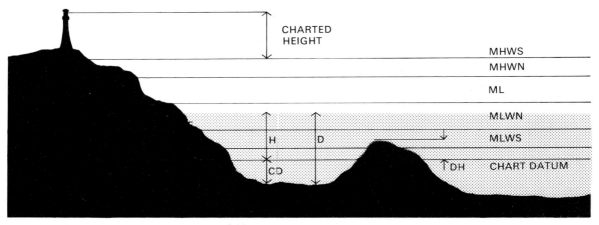

Fig 55. Meaning of terms used in vertical movement of tide. H is depth of water, CD is charted depth, D is depth at the moment when sea level is top of red dotted area, DH is drying height (of the big rock). Other terms abbreviated are mean high water spring tides, mean high water neap tides, mean level, mean low water neap tides and mean low water spring tides.

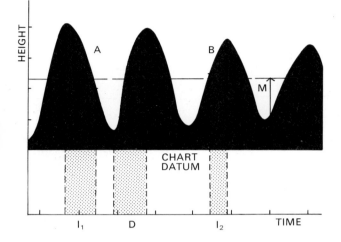

Fig 56. What is meant by various terms in the tidal cycle. Height red wave at any moment is height of tide; M is 'mean level'. There are four high tides here over a couple of days: note how they are a little lower on each high tide. I_1 is 'interval after high water' when tide is at A. I_2 is 'interval before high water' when tide is at B. D is 'duration of mean rise'.

Times at HW and LW are subdivided, the column to use being determined by the time that HW (or LW) occurs at the standard port on the day in question. (Fig 58.)

The daily predictions for each standard port are preceded by tidal curve diagrams showing spring and neap curves. (Figs 57.)

These are used as follows:
Example:
Find the height of the tide at DEVONPORT on July 4th at 1330 BST. From the tide tables extract, Fig 58, find the HW time and height and the LW height. Note that the times are GMT and one hour must be added for BST. All heights are in metres.

	Time	Height
HW	1657	4.8
LW		1.6
Time required	1330	
Interval before HW	0327	
Range this tide		3.2

Find the interval by taking the time required from HW time. Find the range by taking LW height from HW height and compare it with the mean ranges on the tidal curve diagram, Fig 57a (4·7 m springs, 2·2 m neaps). The range for this tide is about halfway between these figures. The continuous curve is for a spring tide and the dashed section for a neap tide. When plotting on the curves it is sufficient to estimate by eye a point between the spring and neap curves if required.

Mark off along the top and bottom height scales, HW and LW heights (4·8 m and 1·6 m) and join these with a range line.

Fill in the HW time (1657) in the appropriate space on the time scale and also mark on the time scale the interval before HW (3h 27 m).

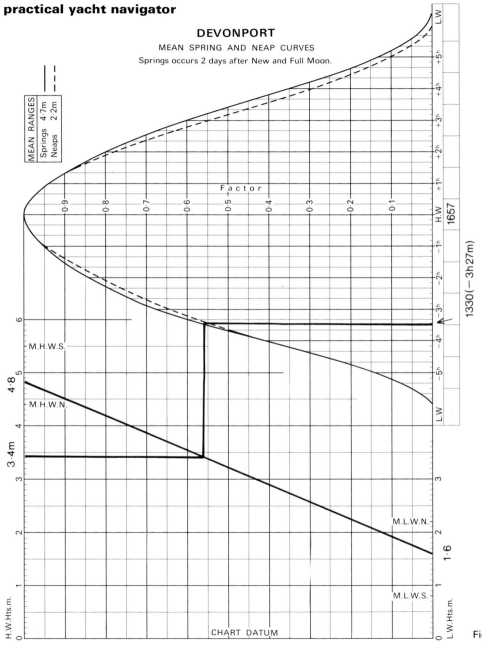

DEVONPORT
MEAN SPRING AND NEAP CURVES
Springs occurs 2 days after New and Full Moon.

Fig 57a.

ENGLAND, SOUTH COAST - PLYMOUTH (DEVONPORT)

LAT 50°22'N   LONG 4°11'W

TIME ZONE **GMT**

TIMES AND HEIGHTS OF HIGH AND LOW WATERS

	JUNE					JULY					AUGUST			
	TIME	M	TIME	M		TIME	M	TIME	M		TIME	M	TIME	M
1 SU	0019 0647 1309 1914	4.5 1.8 4.3 2.0	**16** M	0525 1127 1754 2348	1.8 4.5 2.0 4.7	**1** TU	0019 0651 1304 1919	4.5 1.8 4.4 2.0	**16** W	0555 1156 1826	1.7 4.6 1.8	**1** F	0144 0812 1428 2053	4.2 2.1 4.4 2.1	**16** SA	0138 0807 1427 2056	4.4 2.0 4.6 1.8
2 M	0127 0752 1413 2016	4.6 1.7 4.5 1.8	**17** TU	0636 1238 1908	1.7 4.6 1.8	**2** W	0123 0753 1408 2022	4.5 1.8 4.5 1.9	**17** TH	0023 0707 1313 1944	4.7 1.7 4.6 1.8	**2** SA	0259 0921 1531 2154	4.3 1.9 4.6 1.8	**17** SU	0317 0930 1549 2209	4.5 1.7 4.9 1.4
3 TU	0228 0846 1506 2109	4.7 1.5 4.7 1.6	**18** W	0100 0748 1352 2019	4.8 1.5 4.7 1.6	**3** TH	0228 0852 1506 2121	4.5 1.7 4.7 1.7	**18** F	0146 0824 1435 2102	4.7 1.6 4.7 1.6	**3** SU	0359 1014 1622 2243	4.5 1.7 4.8 1.6	**18** M	0431 1034 1655 2307	4.8 1.3 5.2 1.0
4 W	0319 0934 1549 2156	4.8 1.4 4.9 1.4	**19** TH	0215 0855 1502 2124	4.9 1.3 4.9 1.3	**4** F	0326 0946 1557 2213	4.6 1.6 4.8 1.6	**19** SA	0313 0937 1551 2212	4.7 1.5 4.9 1.3	**4** M	0448 1059 1707 2324	4.6 1.5 5.0 1.4	**19** TU	0531 1127 1751 2356	5.0 1.0 5.4 0.7
5 TH	0403 1018 1629 2239	5.0 1.2 5.1 1.3	**20** F	0327 0956 1606 2224	5.1 1.1 5.1 1.1	**5** SA	0418 1034 1643 2259	4.7 1.4 4.9 1.4	**20** SU	0428 1041 1658 2313	4.9 1.2 5.1 1.0	**5** TU	0531 1138 1747	4.8 1.3 5.1	**20** W	0623 1214 1840	5.3 0.8 5.6
6 F	0444 1059 1708 2320	5.0 1.2 5.1 1.2	**21** SA	0434 1053 1706 2321	5.2 1.0 ·5.3 0.9	**6** SU	0505 1117 1727 2342	4.8 1.4 5.0 1.3	**21** M	0534 1137 1759 ○	5.0 1.0 5.3	**6** W	0002 0610 1215 1824	1.2 4.9 1.2 5.2	**21** TH	0040 0707 1256 1922	0.6 5.4 0.7 5.6

● (below column 5 August)

Fig 58. Part of a page of tide tables for Devonport. New tables are issued each year.

---

302   **ISLES OF SCILLY, AND ENGLAND, SOUTH COAST**

No.	PLACE	Lat. N.	Long. W.	TIME DIFFERENCES High Water (Zone G.M.T.)		Low Water		HEIGHT DIFFERENCES (IN METRES) MHWS	MHWN	MLWN	MLWS	M.L. Z₀ m.
				0000 and 1200	0600 and 1800	0000 and 1200	0600 and 1800					
14	**PLYMOUTH (DEVONPORT)**	(see page 2)		0000 and 1200	0600 and 1800	0000 and 1200	0600 and 1800	5·5	4·4	2·2	0·8	
	England											
	Isles of Scilly											
1	St. Mary's	49 55	6 19	−0030	−0110	−0100	−0020	+0·2	−0·1	−0·2	−0·1	3·13
2	Penzance (Newlyn)	50 06	5 33	−0040	−0105	−0045	−0020	+0·1	0·0	−0·2	0·0	3·08
2a	Porthleven	50 05	5 19	−0045	−0105	−0035	−0025	0·0	−0·1	−0·2	0·0	3·08
3	Lizard Point	49 57	5 12	−0045	−0055	−0040	−0030	−0·2	−0·2	−0·3	−0·2	2·99
4	Coverack	50 01	5 05	−0030	−0040	−0020	−0010	−0·2	−0·2	−0·3	−0·2	2·99
4a	Helford River (Entrance)	50 05	5 05	−0030	−0035	−0015	−0010	−0·2	−0·2	−0·3	−0·2	⊙

Fig 59. Details of secondary port related to a standard port.

Draw a line upwards from the interval to a point halfway between the spring and neap curves.

From this position, draw a line to the left to intersect the range line and then upwards to the height scale.

Read off the height which is 3·4 m.

Example:
Find the time that the tide will first rise to a height of 2·0 m at DEVONPORT on August 21st.

Extract the HW time and height and LW height and find the range as before. Establish whether it is a spring or a neap tide.

	Time	Height
HW	0807	5·4
LW		0·6
Range this tide		4·8 (springs)
Height required	2m	

Mark off the height scales as before and draw the range line.

Enter the HW time in the time scale. (Fig 57b.)

Mark off 2·0 m on the HW height scale and draw a line downwards to the range line and then to the right to intersect the spring curve on the rising tide.

From this point draw a line down to the time scale and read off the interval and the time (4 h 27 m before HW = 0340 BST).

Devonport is a standard port. For all standard ports HW and LW times and heights are tabulated, but for secondary ports a little more work is required.

To find the time and height of HW and LW at a secondary port, the differences for the secondary port are applied to the predictions for the related standard port, Fig 59.

Example:
Find the times and heights of HW and LW at ST. MARY'S, ISLES OF SCILLY, in the afternoon of June 1st (standard port, Devonport). (Fig 59.)

At standard port, Devonport

	Time		Height	
	HW	LW	HW	LW
(leave times in GMT)	1309	1914	4·3	2·0

Determine differences:

When at standard port,
HW is at 1200, difference is −0030
1800, difference is −0110
Interpolated for 1309, difference = −0038

When at standard port,
LW is at 1800, difference is −0020
0000, difference is −0100
Interpolated for 1914, difference = −0028

When at standard port,
HW is 5·5, difference is +0·2
4·4, difference is −0·1
Interpolation for 4·3, difference is −0·1

When at standard port
LW is 2·2, difference is −0·2
0·8, difference is −0·1
Interpolation for 2·0, difference is −0·2

Standard Port Devonport

	Time		Height	
	HW	LW	HW	LW
Devonport GMT	1309	1914	4·3	2·0
Differences	−0038	−0028	−0·1	−0·2
St. Mary's GMT	1231	1846	4·2	1·8
Add 1 hour BST	1331	1946		

In practice interpolation by eye is usually sufficient

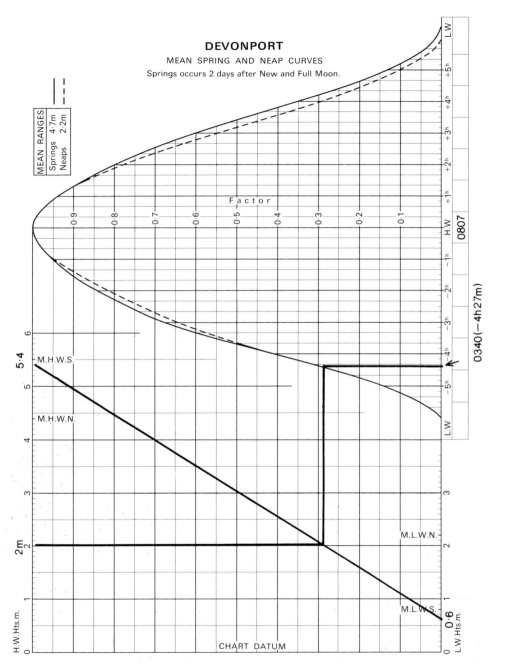

Fig 57b.

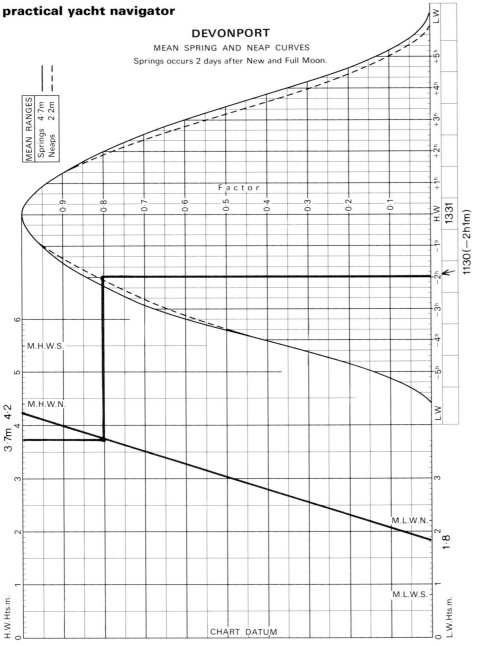

DEVONPORT

MEAN SPRING AND NEAP CURVES
Springs occurs 2 days after New and Full Moon.

MEAN RANGES
Springs 4·7m
Neaps 2·2m

Factor

0·9 0·8 0·7 0·6 0·5 0·4 0·3 0·2 0·1

+5ʰ
+4ʰ
+3ʰ
+2ʰ
+1ʰ
H.W 1331
−1ʰ
−2ʰ
−3ʰ
−4ʰ
−5ʰ
L.W

1130(−2h1m)

M.H.W.S.
M.H.W.N.
M.L.W.N.
M.L.W.S.

CHART DATUM

H.W.Hts.m.
L.W.Hts.m.

3·7m 4·2
1·8

Fig 57c.

To find the height of tide at a secondary port at intermediate times between HW and LW, the times and heights of HW and LW at the secondary port are found, as in the previous example, and entered on the tidal curve diagram for the standard port (There are special cases for which the secondary port curves differ significantly from the standard port curve. These require a special procedure which is fully explained in the Admiralty Tide Table). The standard port range is used to determine whether it is a spring or neap tide.

Example:
Find the height of tide at ST. MARY'S, ISLES OF SCILLY, at 1130 BST on June 1st.

From previous example,

		Time	Height	
St Mary's	HW	1331	4·2	
	LW		1·8	
Time required		1130		
Interval before HW		0201		

Devonport range 2·3 (neaps)

Enter the HW time and height and the LW height on the Devonport tidal curve diagram and proceed as for the previous examples. The height found is 3·7 m. The procedure to find the time at which the height of tide will be at a given level at a secondary port is similar to the standard port example (page 106).

Special Solent Curves

For ports between Swanage and Selsey including the Solent, shallow water effects cause double high waters or tidal stands at HW of up to two hours. This makes it difficult to define the exact time of HW. The tidal differences also vary markedly between these two ports. As a result, tidal curves for most secondary ports are referred to LW.

The procedure for using the LW tidal curve diagrams is similar to that used for the HW diagrams except that each secondary port has its own curve. These curves are entered with secondary port times and heights based on standard port times and heights at Portsmouth. (Fig 61a.)
In the examples secondary corrections have been found from the extract from Reed's Nautical Almanac, Figs 60a & b.

Example:
Find the height of tide at YARMOUTH at 1330 BST on May 23rd.
Standard port Portsmouth

		Time	Height
Portsmouth	HW		4·7
	LW	1558 GMT	0·6
	Range		4·1 (springs)

Using Reed's 'Tidal Differences on Portsmouth' table Fig 60b enter Mean Low Water (MLW) column opposite Yarmouth:

LW time difference is −25 mins
LW height difference is −0·2

enter Mean High Water (MHW) column:
HW height difference is −1·4 m

	Time		Height
	LW	HW	LW
Portsmouth	1558 GMT	4·7	0·6
Differences	−0025	−1·4	−0·2
Yarmouth	1533 GMT	3·3	0·4
Add 1 hour for BST	1633 BST		

PORTSMOUTH

HIGH & LOW WATER GMT

**ADD 1 HOUR MARCH 30—
OCTOBER 25 FOR B.S.T.**

Fig 60a.

MAY

TIME	M		TIME	M
1 0420	3.9	**16**	0331	3.7
TH 0949	1.5	F	0852	1.6
1727	3.9		1621	3.7
2237	1.9		2133	1.9
2 0544	3.7	**17**	0434	3.6
F 1118	1.6	SA	0959	1.7
1855	3.9		1730	3.7
			2250	1.9
3 0009	1.8	**18**	0548	3.6
SA 0714	3.7	SU	1116	1.6
1242	1.5		1841	3.9
2008	4.0			
4 0122	1.6	**19**	0003	1.7
SU 0823	3.8	M	0700	3.8
1344	1.3		1225	1.4
2102	4.2		1942	4.1
5 0215	1.3	**20**	0103	1.4
M 0914	4.0	TU	0800	4.0
1431	1.1		1324	1.1
2143	4.4		2036	4.4
6 0256	1.1	**21**	0156	1.1
TU 0955	4.2	W	0854	4.3
1510	0.9		1418	0.8
2218	4.5		2125	4.6
7 0331	1.0	**22**	0244	0.8
W 1030	4.4	TH	0945	4.6
1546	0.9		1508	0.7
2251	4.6		2214	4.8
8 0404	0.9	**23**	0331	0.7
TH 1106	4.5	F	1035	4.7
● 1621	0.9		1558	0.6
2323	4.6	O	2303	4.9
9 0437	0.8	**24**	0419	0.5
F 1141	4.5	SA	1127	4.8
1656	0.9		1645	0.6
2356	4.5		2350	4.9

Fig 60b.

TIDAL DIFFERENCES ON PORTSMOUTH

PLACE	MHW		MLW		GUIDING DEPTH AT			
	Tm. Diff.	Ht. Diff.	Tm. Diff.	Ht. Diff.	HWS	HWN	CD	POSITION
	h. min.	m.	h. min.	m.	m.	m.	m.	
Yarmouth	− 1 05S + 0 05N	− 1.4	− 0 25	− 0.2	5.0	4.4	1.9	Castle Pier
Totland Bay	− 1 30S − 0 45N	− 1.8	− 0 40	− 0.3	4.3	3.9	1.6	Pier head
Alum Bay	− 1 40S − 0 50N	− 1.8	− 0 40	− 0.3	—	—	—	Anchorage prohibited
The Solent Hurst Point	− 1 15S − 0 05N	− 1.7	− 0 25	− 0.3	10.7	10.3	8.0	Hurst Road
Keyhaven	− 1 05S 0 00N	− 1.6	− 0 25	− 0.3	6.6	6.1	3.7	In Lake behind bar
Lymington	− 0 55S + 0 05N	− 1.5	− 0 20	− 0.3	4.4	4.0	1.4	Bar

Enter the low water tidal curve diagram for Yarmouth. Fig 61a with LW time and height and HW height and draw in the range. Next, locate the required time 1330 (− 3 hr 3 mins LW Portsmouth) and descend to the curve representing springs. Then rule horizontally to cut the days range and read off the height above which is 2·9 m.

Example:
Find the time at LYMINGTON on May 2nd when the height of the morning tide falls to 1·5 m.

		Time	Height
Portsmouth	HW		3·7
	LW	1118 GMT	1·6
	Range		2·1 (neaps)

LW time difference is − 20 mins
LW height difference is − 0·3
HW height difference is − 1·5

	Time		Height	
	LW	HW		LW
Portsmouth	1118			
	GMT	3·7		1·6
Differences	−20	−1·5		−0·3
Lymington	1058			
	GMT	2·2		1·3
Add 1 hour				
for BST	1158			
	BST			

Height required 1·5 m

Enter the tidal curve for Lymington, Fig 61b, with LW time and height and then HW height. Descend from the required height to the days range and rule horizontally to the neap curve. The required time is −50 min (LW Portsmouth) or 1108 BST.

Note: The secondary port corrections shown in Reed's Nautical Almanac are simpler to apply than those in Admiralty Tide Tables. In cases where the difference between the 'differences' (of times and heights) for spring and neap tides is small, then a mean value has been taken.

Whatever method is used to calculate height of tide, a clearance of at least 0·5 m should be allowed between the keel and the seabed. If mean values are used then this should be increased.

The 'Rule of Twelve' method

The assumption is made that the tide rises and falls between LW and HW at a rate proportional to the time between LW and HW. This is by no means always the case, but this method can be used when only a rough approximation is considered adequate, and when no danger can arise if the answer is inaccurate. (Fig 62.)

The rule assumes that

the rise or fall in first hour is	1/12th
second	2/12
third	3/12
fourth	3/12
fifth	2/12
sixth	1/12

of the range of the particular tide.

It works like this. (Fig 63.) Find the approximate height of tide at 1200 at a place and on the day when
HW is at 1000, height 14 ft
LW is at 1615, height   4 ft
Range this tide is 10 ft (14 − 4 ft)
Interval between HW and time required is 2 hours
In first hour, tide falls by   1/12th of range
In second hour, tide falls by 2/12th of range

$$3/12\text{th, or}$$
$$1/4 \text{ of } 10 \text{ ft} = \quad 2.5$$
subtract from HW height of   14·0

Approximate height of tide
at 1200 will be   11·5 ft

There is little to commend the 'Rule of twelve' method as it takes some time to compute it properly, and it is still necessary to look up the daily predictions.

Other methods

Tide Tables produced by other countries usually contain tables for calculating heights at

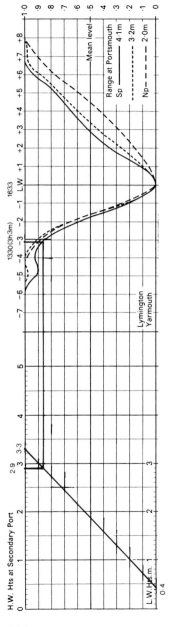

Fig 61a.

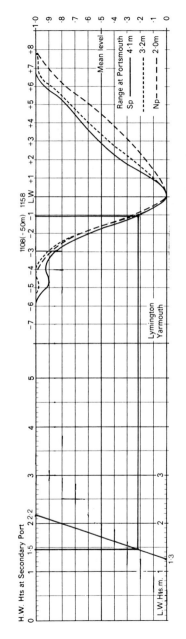

Fig 61b.

intermediate times and give instructions for their use, and examples.

General comments

Tidal calculations inevitably take a little time to work out and check. Heights of tide should therefore be calculated BEFORE they are required, whenever possible. It often saves trouble if the height is worked out for the time it is expected to be required (give or take a few minutes), AND at the same time to work it out for one or more hours before and after this time. If then arrival time is appreciably earlier, or later than the ETA, the figure is ready. It takes very little longer to work the others out once the data has been assembled on paper.

Always allow a margin for safety, both in depth (assume depth may be less than that calculated) and in time (assume tide may be later in coming up to a required height, or may be early in falling to a given height).

Tidal streams do not by any means always reverse their direction at high or low water, but may do so some hours earlier or later. The tidal atlas or tidal information in the panel on the chart must be consulted. The range of the tide does, however, give good guidance as to the probable rates of the tidal stream as between the rate shown at springs and neaps respectively.

Whenever a height of tide problem is not clear, make a rough sketch showing chart datum level, level of water, chart depth and so on, as in the illustrations given here.

Having checked a calculation (and never use one until it has been checked), stand back and see if it 'looks sensible'. Often an error in principle comes to light this way.

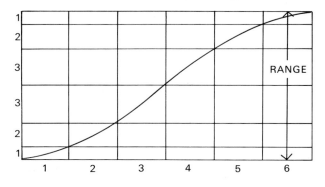

Fig 62. The 'rule of twelve' assumes that a tide rises on this pattern. Numbers on left are twelfths of the range for the day, bottom numbers are a succession of hours. Reference to local tide graphs shows many exceptions.

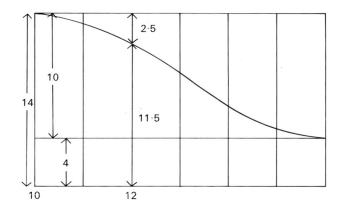

Fig 63. The example of how to use the rule of twelve.

9. This is the position

Plotting the yacht's position is the basis of coastal navigation. The snag is that it is subject to small but accumulative errors. To wipe these out at one stroke, it is necessary to obtain a fix.

Within sight of land, this fix is found by reference to objects such as lighthouses, conspicuous buildings, headlands, light vessels and buoys. A radio beacon comes into the same category.

To be of any value for finding the yacht's position an object must meet TWO conditions:

(a) The object must be POSITIVELY IDENTIFIED.
(b) The same object must be identifiable on the chart.

This point cannot be overstressed. Many yachts—and commercial vessels—have come to grief entirely due to mistaking one object for another, either visually or on the chart. A lighthouse seen at night must be positively identified by the characteristics of its light. A buoy is similarly identified by night, and by day (particularly if there are several buoys around) its exact name should be read. Care needs taking in finding the correct buoy on the chart. Many have rather similar names. A lighthouse on a headland seen by day can be mistaken for another, and calls for careful verification by studying the contours of the land near it and comparing with those on the chart.

A single observation of a single identifiable object will provide a position *line*—and only a position line—somewhere along which is the yacht's position. To obtain a positive fix, two (or more) objects must be observed almost simultaneously. However, there are occasions when even a single observation of a single object can be of real value. Position lines can be obtained by finding either the bearing of an object, or its range. Occasionally both bearing and range of one object can be found, in which case a fix is possible. To be precise, the range of an object will provide a circle of position (as opposed to a position line), that is, a circle round the object somewhere on the circumference of which the observer's position must lie.

The methods of position line finding are:
(a) Bearing Methods.
By compass bearing.
RDF bearing.
Transit of two objects in line.
Radar bearing.
(b) Range Methods.
By rising and dipping distance of a lighthouse.
Vertical sextant angle of an object of known height.
Horizontal sextant angle of two (or more) objects.
Radar range.
Soundings (in some circumstances).

Any one of these will provide a position line (or circle of position from ranges), and any two will provide a fix (if the position lines cross at a suitably wide angle). Circumstances will normally dictate which of all these methods should be used.

By compass bearing

A position line from observation of a single identifiable object can be established by taking a compass bearing of it. From the object on the chart, lay off a line in the direction of the reciprocal of its bearing from the yacht. If a hand bearing compass is used, either lay off in relation to the magnetic rose on the chart, or convert the compass bearing to true and lay off in relation to the meridians on the chart, for instance, (Reciprocal = Bearing + or − 180°).

(a) Bearing of object from ship 046°T
PL from object   226°T
(b) Bearing of object from ship 315°T
PL from object   135°T
or, Bearing from ship 127°M
Variation   8°W
$\overline{}$
119°T, reciprocal = 299°T

(When using a Douglas protractor for this purpose, a useful tip is to orientate the centre hole of the protractor over the *object* and the lines parallel with a meridian, but with the north point downwards (to S). Then use the original true bearing from ship to object to lay off the position line. This saves the conversion to a reciprocal bearing—and eliminates one possible source of error).

By a transit

If two identifiable objects are seen one behind the other in transit, then a compass bearing is unnecessary. The yacht must be on a line extending seawards and passing through both objects. When it presents itself this provides an accurate position line as it eliminates any compass error.

This is of particular value when entering (or leaving) a port. In Fig 64 a current of unknown strength is setting across the entrance. By watching the transit the helmsman can keep on the line, heading up towards the current a little more, or less, so that the objects appear to remain stationary.

Cross bearings

If TWO objects can be identified both visually and on the chart, then a position line from each can be obtained by compass bearing. (Fig 65.) Since the yacht must be on both position lines, the intersection of the two lines must be her position, provided always that the bearings are accurately observed and plotted. Note that the nearer the observed objects are, the smaller will be the error in the position resulting from an error in the bearing taken. (Fig 66.) The more nearly the two objects subtend an angle of 90° the better the 'cut' (Fig 67.).

If three identifiable objects can be observed and their bearings taken, the resulting position lines should cross at a point. They seldom do so exactly, but form a triangle or 'cocked hat', the size of which gives a guide as to the reliability of the observations. If the cocked hat is of appreciable size one or more of the bearings are inaccurate. This may be due to

(a) One or more of the objects observed not being the one on the chart.
(b) Error in taking one or more of the bearings.
(c) Variation wrongly applied or wrong.
(d) Simply an error in laying off the position lines on the chart.

The odds on the true position being inside the

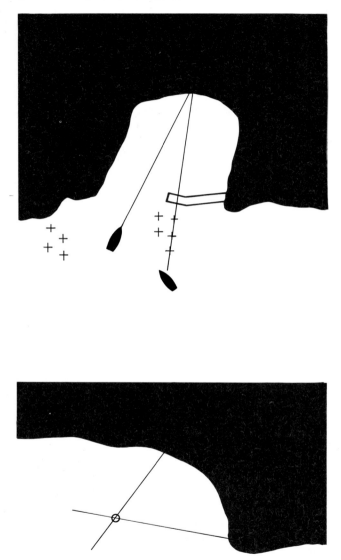

Fig 64. Properly identified transit points provide best checks for keeping on a position line. If stream is setting across, yacht can still be maintained on correct line by heading up slightly.

Fig 65. Simple fix from two objects on land. If bearings are reliable, yacht is at intersection.

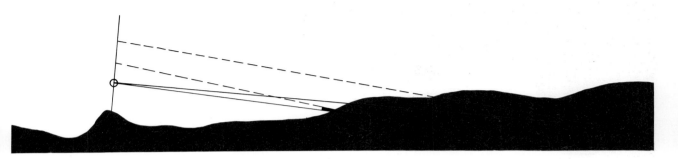

Fig 66. Nearer objects are more reliable for bearings. Here same angular error on distant object gives twice the error in position.

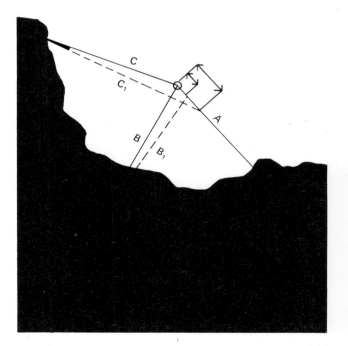

Fig 67. Bearings A and B make a good angle of cut. A and C make a bad angle. Note that error B gives only one third of position change of error C_1. This is because of wide angle of C–C_1 to A.

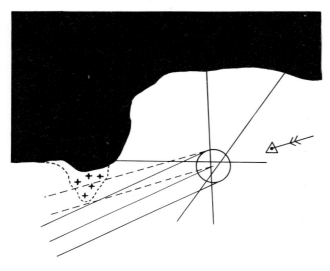

Fig 68. Cross bearings giving indeterminate position. Subsequent course as given by dotted lines could result in hitting rocks. Solid line courses in south westerly direction will all clear dangers, wherever yacht is in circle.

Fig 69. Two position lines taken when the yacht is moving along a known course and distance. Estimated position was EP and fix was obtained after second position line had been obtained.

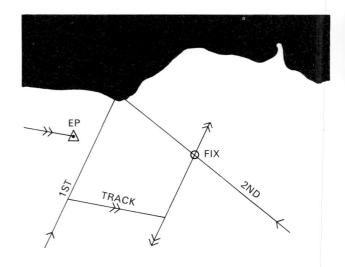

cocked hat are four to one against. Do not therefore assume that the true position is bound to be inside the triangle, but draw a rough circle round its centre of diameter somewhat greater than the longest side. If the triangle is large, then re-check all working. (Fig 68)

Running fix

If only one identifiable object is visible, a good approximation of the yacht's position can be obtained by taking one compass bearing of it, followed by a second one when the bearing of the original object has changed substantially, and yacht has moved a known distance in a known direction. The position when the second bearing was taken can be found by simple geometry.

Both position lines are plotted in the usual way. Then the first position line is transferred forward in the direction and the distance travelled *over the ground* since the first bearing was taken. (Fig 69.) If there is no tidal stream, the procedure is simply

Take the first bearing and read the log.

Keep yacht on a steady compass course and note course steered.

When bearing of object has changed by about 40° or more, take a second bearing of it; read the log.

Plot both bearings as position lines.

From any point on first position line draw a line in the direction of ship's water track (heading corrected for leeway) of length equal to the miles run between bearings, as recorded by log. Through the end of this line draw a line parallel to the first position line. This is the 'transferred position line'.

Where transferred PL crosses the second PL is the ship's position when the second bearing was taken.

The accuracy of the running fix depends on the correctness of the direction and distance travelled *over the ground* between the two

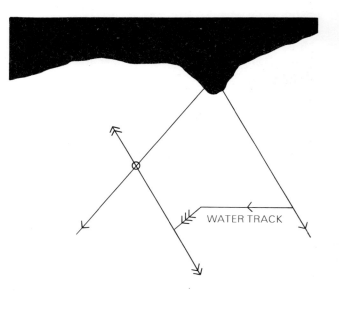

Fig 70.   Validity of running fix depends on correct allowance for tidal stream or current (treble arrowed line). Water track alone is not sufficient. Transferred PL (double arrows) cuts second bearing to give fix (small circle).

bearings, as well as upon the accuracy of the two bearings taken.

Reference to the appropriate page in the tidal stream atlas (or to a conveniently near tide 'diamond' on the chart) will show what the tidal stream was doing (Fig 70.). If there is such a stream, this must be plotted on from the water track so that the true direction and distance the yacht has moved over the ground—her track—between the times of the two bearings is plotted.

To find the distance off without plotting

Two methods of finding the distance from a single object without plotting are of interest. These are of limited value as their accuracy depends on knowing the distance and direction sailed *over the ground* between taking two bearings of the one object. This will of course be affected by any tidal stream.

Tidal streams off headlands, where the distance off is often required, are difficult to predict and are often strong. Few charts or tidal stream atlases show the tidal stream close in with any accuracy, and the stream may well be setting at a different rate or direction from the nearest point of tide reference. These methods also require the bearing to be taken at frequent intervals, which is not always convenient. For these reasons, these methods should only be used when the stream is known to be slack or negligible, and the result should be used with caution and ample margins for safety allowed.

Doubling the angle on the bow

1. A first bearing of the object is taken and converted to a relative bearing, to give the angle between the ship's head and the object. The log is read, and noted.
2. The object is watched, and when the relative bearing is exactly twice the first relative bearing

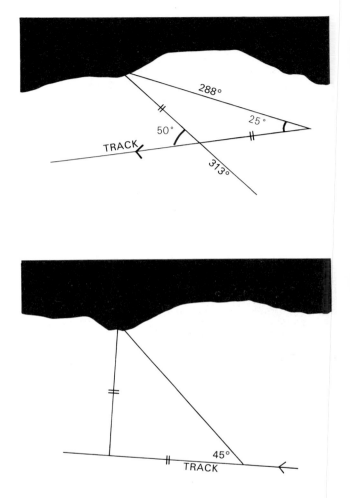

Fig 71. Doubling the angle on the bow. When the angle of the object against the ship's head is doubled then the distance off equals the distance run, which therefore has to be accurately known. Red angle is double black angle.

Fig 72. A four point bearing doubles the angle of the bow when it is 45° to give a distance off when the object is exactly abeam.

the log is read again.

3. The distance run between the two bearings is the same as the distance from the object when the second bearing was taken. (Figs 71 and 72.)

Position finding by sextant

In addition to its primary use for celestial observations, the sextant is of great value to the coastal navigator. It can be used to measure the horizontal angle subtended at the observer between any two objects, or to measure the vertical angle subtended between an object of known height and sea level below it.

Horizontal sextant angles

If the sextant is held flat, (i.e. the plane of the arc horizontal, handle downward, mirrors upward) the index arm can be moved so that the direct image of one object and the reflected image of a second object to its right, are superimposed on each other. The sextant reading gives the exact angle subtended between the two objects. The objects are more easily seen if the telescope is removed.

If the two objects are marked on the chart, knowing the angle between them will enable a circle to be drawn which will cut both objects (Fig 73.); the observer will be somewhere on the circumference of this circle. This is a circle of position, but without some further evidence it is not possible to say at what point on the circumference is the observer's position.

If however, a third object can be identified and its angle from one of the first two objects measured, a second circle of position can be drawn (Fig 74.), and the observer's position is then fixed at the intersection of the two circumferences—because this is now the only point on one circle of position which is also on the other circle.

A 'fix' by HSA of three objects is likely to be

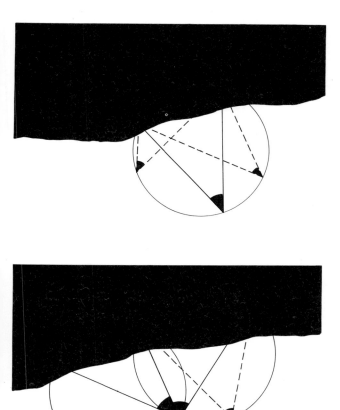

Fig 73. A single horizontal angle gives a circular position line. Like any position line this can be crossed with a single bearing, radio signal, soundings or similar line.

Fig 74. If horizontal sextant angles can be taken using three objects, this is the most accurate way of obtaining a fix from them. Station pointer can be used for quick results.

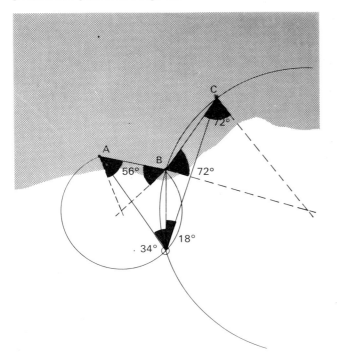

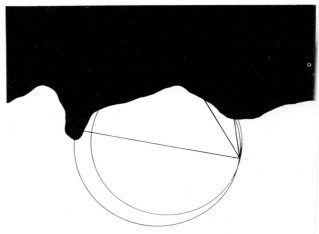

Fig 77. When centre object in on far side of outer one, satisfactory results are not obtained with horizontal sextant angles.

Fig 75. The horizontal sextant angles between A and B, and between B and C are: A 34° B 18° C. From each base line A–B and B–C, lay off lines making the compliment of the measured angle (90°–34°=56°, and 90°–18°=72°.)

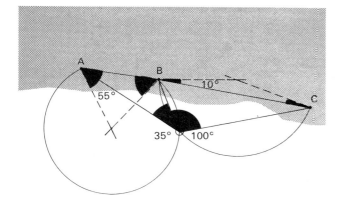

Fig 76. Plotting angles when one horizontal sextant angle exceeds 90°.

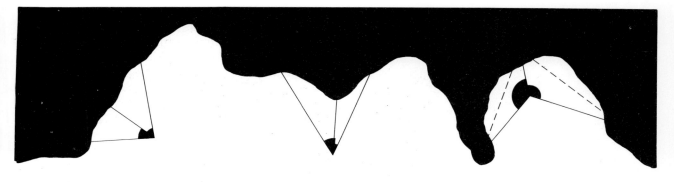

Fig 78. Different situations when plotting with station pointer which meet the requirements which have been listed.

more accurate than one by compass bearings because the angles found by sextant can be extremely accurate, and compass error cannot arise.

The 'fix' by HSA of three objects can be established on the chart in several ways:
(a) By calculating and plotting the circles on the chart.
(b) By the use of a station pointer.
(c) By using tracing paper or a Douglas protractor on chart.

By plotting
Assume the angles between three objects are found by sextant to be: 34° between A and B, 18° between B and C. This is normally written: 'A 34° B 18° C.'

Rule a straight line between A and B. From A, lay off a line making an angle from the line A–B of the *complement* of the observed angle (90°— obs. angle = 56°. The intersection of the lines just drawn gives the centre of the first circle. Describe the circle to cut both A and B. Repeat the process for the angle between B and the third object C. (Fig 75.) (90°—18° = 72°.)

If the observed angle is *greater* than 90°, subtract 90° from observed angle and lay off the lines on the opposite (landward) side of the line joining the two objects. (Fig 76.)

By station pointer
This is a circular protractor engraved for 0°–180° to left and right of 0°; it has a central arm fixed at 0°, and two other arms, pivoted at the centre, which can be moved and locked into position subtending any required angle from the centre arm. The arms are set to the angles found by sextant, the centre arm placed on the chart to cut the central object, and the whole instrument is then moved around till the bevelled edge of each arm cuts its respective object. (Fig 80.) There is a hole through the central pivot. A pencil point through this hole will mark the observed position.

This is quite the quickest method of plotting a fix by two horizontal sextant angles. There is now an inexpensive clear plastic station pointer which works well, and also has calibrations on it for obtaining distances off by vertical sextant angle (see below). This is the Ebbco combined station pointer and distance-off calculator.

By tracing paper or Douglas protractor

If no Station Pointer is available it is quite simple to mark the necessary angles and lines on any transparent material. Draw a central vertical line. From the lower end of this line draw lines to left and right, each making the required angle from the central line. Move the paper or protractor round till each line cuts its respective object. With a compass point stab the intersection point of the three lines on the transparent paper or protractor through to the chart. When using a Douglas protractor, lay off the lines on reversed sides of the central line, then turn the protractor over, face down. The lines then show up much more clearly.

The selection of suitable objects for horizontal sextant angles is important. They must be chosen so that :

(a) The three objects are all on, or near, the same straight line, or

(b) The centre object is on the near side of a line joining the two outer objects, or

(c) The ship's position is clearly inside a triangle formed by joining the three objects.

These provisos are to ensure that the circumferences of the two circles intersect at a good angle of 'cut', and to avoid ambiguity. (Fig 78.)

By plotting—without compasses

A quick way, which only requires a protractor, is as follows : Join A to B and B to C by straight lines. From B, lay off a line BV, angle ABV being the complement (90°-angle) of the horizontal sextant angle. From A, draw a line at right angles to AB, to cut BV at X. Repeat the process from C, angle CBW being the complement of the horizontal sextant angle, the line at right angles to BC cutting BW at Y. Join X and Y. Drop a perpen-dicular from B to XY to Z. Z is the fix. (Fig 79a.) (If the horizontal sextant angle is greater than 90°, subtract 90° from it and lay off on landward side.) (Fig 79b.)

If a sextant is not available, the angular difference between bearings can be used in the same way. This is a useful method to check deviation as it is not necessary to convert compass bearings to true to plot them as the angular difference is the same. When the position is found by one of the methods already mentioned any one of the three compass bearings can be compared with the true bearing and after variation has been applied any remaining difference is deviation for the yacht's heading.

Fig 79a.   Horizontal sextant angles are 40° and 35°.

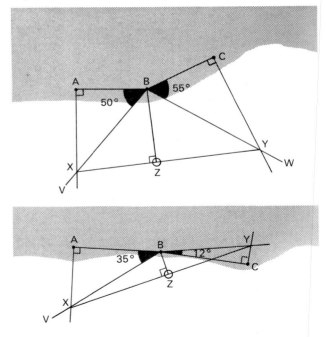

Fig 79b.   Horizontal sextant angles are 55° and 102°.

THE STATION POINTER

Some station pointers have, instead of a hole for pencil, a dimple or point on the underside at the centre. Pressure on the instrument produces an impression on the chart which can be made bolder by a pencil mark. In suitable cases, positions can be plotted more quickly, and with

Ebbco station pointer with single fixed arm and two that can be revolved and then clamped. It incorporates a quick calculation for distance by vertical sextant angle.

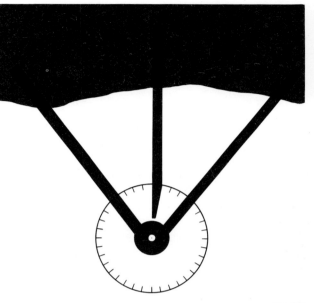

Fig 80.

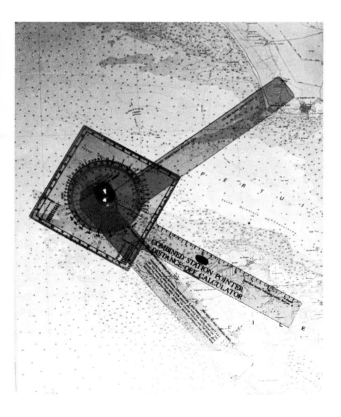

greater accuracy by this method than is possible by taking compass bearings of objects. A useful tip when moving the station pointer to align each arm over its respective object on the chart is to place a compass point (or divider point) on the centre object. The centre arm of the station pointer is then steadied against the compass point and the instrument is slid around till left and right hand arms are both aligned over their respective objects—the compass point ensuring that the centre arm is also correctly positioned.

127

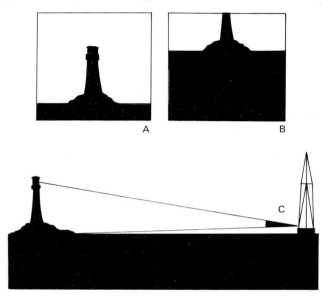

Fig 81. Set sextant so direct and reflected images almost coincide (A). Then (B and C) measure angle between sea level at lighthouse and lantern.

Vertical sextant angle

If you can see, and identify, a lighthouse, beacon or any object the height of which is marked on the chart, and you can also see the foreshore immediately below the object, then your distance off the object (its range) can be found immediately, and very accurately, by measuring its height with the sextant and consulting the 'Distance by vertical sextant angle' given in Burton's Tables, Norie's Nautical Tables or Reed's Nautical Almanac.

The sextant should be set at approximately zero degrees. Both the direct and the reflected image of, say, the L/H will be seen in the telescope, superimposed one on the other. Adjust the sextant so that the lantern of the right-hand (reflected) image is bisected by the horizon (sea line) of the direct image. Read the sextant and correct the reading for any index error. (Fig 81.)

Enter the table with the height of the lighthouse (from chart or light list).

Follow down the 'height' column till the angle found by the sextant is reached. The Distance-off is found in the left or right hand column. Here is an example.

Dungeness lighthouse (4·0 m)	
Sextant altitude	0° 19'
Index error	− 2'
True angle	0° 17'

Distance-off 4·4 miles (see Table. Fig 82.)

If a compass bearing is taken at the same time, an absolute 'fix' is obtained; the bearing giving the position line, and the angle giving the distance-off, measured along this line.

Note that the point at sea level immediately below the object must be within your horizon. If your height of eye is about 7 ft or less, this means that distance-off calculations of objects beyond 3 miles cannot be accurately determined.

DISTANCE BY VERTICAL ANGLE

Height of Object

Distance mls		38.5	40
	m	38.5	40
	ft	126	131
		° '	° '
4.0		0 18	0 19
.2		0 17	0 18
.4		0 16	0 17
.6		0 16	0 16
.8		0 15	0 15

Fig 82.

Fig 83. Heights of lights are given for mean high water springs, so charted height is H1 and not H2 which represents the sea level at any given moment. (CD is chart datum from which height is not given). Example shows navigator taking vertical sextant angle when sea level is 3.0 m below MHWS. Lighthouse height is 31 m and his reading of 29′ gives distance of 2 miles (A), but really (R) he is 2.2 miles. When dangers are inshore of yacht this is an additional safety (but not in the case of Fig 84, maximum distance).

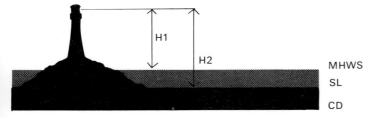

MHWS

SL

CD

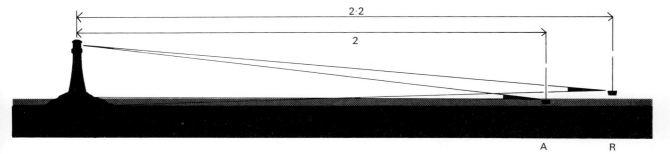

practical yacht navigator

It will be remembered that all heights of objects not periodically covered by sea (e.g. lanterns of lighthouses) are shown on the charts as heights above MHWS. If at the time the tide is below MHWS the amount it is so below must be ADDED to the charted height. If this point is neglected, the true distance off will be something *more* than that calculated. This is usually insignificant, but if the distance off is being used to ensure not passing too *far* off (as when passing *inside* a danger), then the necessary correction should be applied. To make the correction for height of tide, calculate the height of tide at the time (Fig 83.), ascertain the height of tide at MHWS, subtract the former from the latter and add this to the charted height of the object.

Danger angles

If the course lies past a lighthouse with offlying dangers the sextant may be used to ensure that a minimum distance is maintained from it in order to clear the danger. If the appropriate danger angle is set on the sextant (entering the table with minimum distance-off required height) then as soon as the VSA observed approaches (increases up to) the danger angle, course can be altered away from the object to the extent necessary to keep the angle on the sextant less than the danger angle. (Fig 84.)

Rising and dipping distances

A useful method of finding one's distance from a lighthouse at night is by observing when the light first appears above the horizon when approaching, or first disappears when receding from, the lighthouse. Usually the loom of the lighthouse is first seen when the light is below the horizon, often long before the actual light can be seen. If the height of the light is known, a table of rising and dipping distances will give the

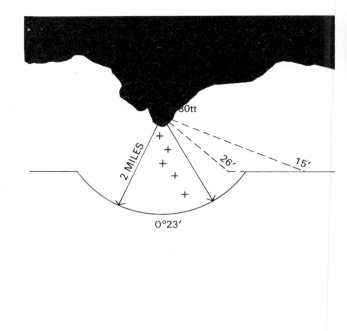

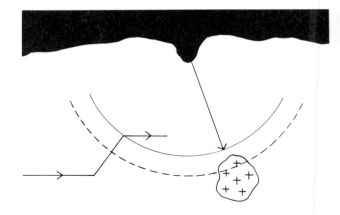

Fig 84.   Minimum safe distance off given by vertical sextant angle. A lighthouse of 25 m at 2 miles gives 0° 23'. Diagram shows readings at different places. Below, same principle is applied to a maximum safe distance, though a decision is needed on when to enter 'maximum circle'.

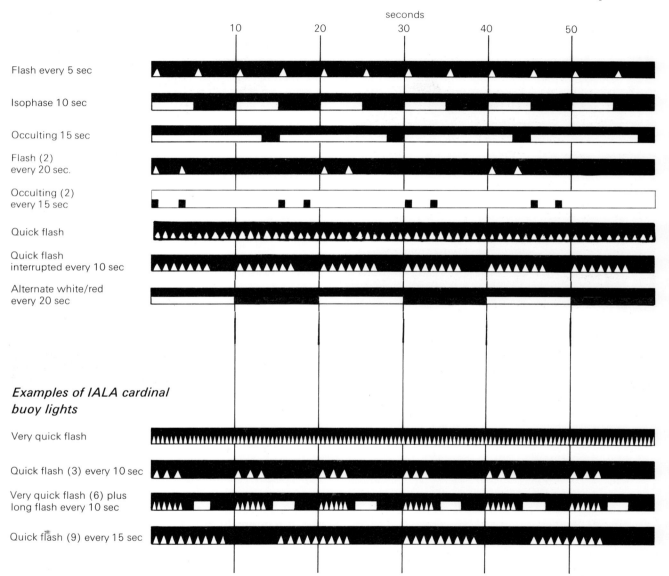

Flash every 5 sec

Isophase 10 sec

Occulting 15 sec

Flash (2)
every 20 sec.

Occulting (2)
every 15 sec

Quick flash

Quick flash
interrupted every 10 sec

Alternate white/red
every 20 sec

*Examples of IALA cardinal
buoy lights*

Very quick flash

Quick flash (3) every 10 sec

Very quick flash (6) plus
long flash every 10 sec

Quick flash (9) every 15 sec

Fig 85. Characteristics of the lights of navigational marks. Buoys in proximity will each have a pattern to avoid confusion with others nearby. The same applies to lighthouses that can be seen from a single position. Remember a stop watch must be used when timing these. The chart or almanac will give the time interval for a particular light. This period is timed from the beginning of one pattern to the beginning of the next. It would be the same thing to take the time from the finish of a cycle.

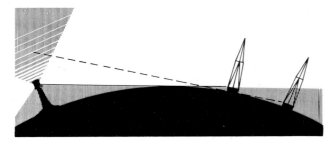

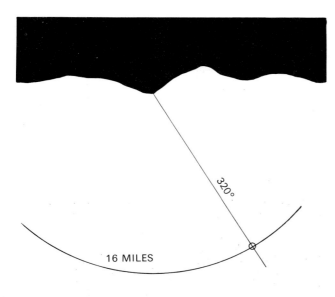

320°

16 MILES

Fig 86. As explained, care must be taken before relying on dipping light for a fix. In top picture, light is just visible to left yacht, but from deck of right yacht only the loom can be seen Navigator on his chart has drawn radius for distance of light 'just dipping' and crossed with a compass bearing of the light to get a fix.

distance off at the moment the light is on the horizon.

This will provide a valuable method of position fixing when approaching a coast. Calculation of the distance off provides a circle of position, and a compass bearing a position line crossing the circle. (Fig 86.) To be of any value—

(a) The loom must be seen before the actual light appears (when approaching) or after it disappears (when receding).
(b) The light must be positively identified by its characteristics.
(c) The distance off must be taken for the actual height of eye of the observer.

The light flashes should be counted and timed with a stopwatch for several periods of the light. If some counts and times are not exactly repeated (e.g. 4 flashes every 30 sec), continue counting and timing until they are. Stress is laid on this point as many navigators have assumed that inconsistencies (e.g. sometimes 3 flashes, sometimes 4) were due to wave interference, and have allowed 'wishful thinking' to persuade them they have identified the hoped-for light when in fact it is another—or even a distant ship's light being obscured and visible as she, or the yacht, rises and falls on the waves.

The range of a light first seen on approaching s limited by either
(a) Height of observer's eye and height of light, above sea level, due to the earth's curvature, (which gives its geographical range), or by
(b) the intensity of the light if not powerful, (called its 'nominal range').

This is why it is important to look for the loom before (on approach) or after (on leaving) seeing the actual light. If this is not spotted due to poor visibility or due to it being a weak light, it might first be seen when it was actually above the horizon, and thus much nearer than its geographical range.

Distance off a light just rising or dipping is most accurately found by entering the table in Reed's, Norie's or Burton's Tables with (a) Height of Eye and (b) Height of light, which determine respectively: (a) distance from observer to horizon and (b) distance from horizon to light. A light's height is shown against it on a large-scale chart and in lists of lights.

There is an important difference in the information about lights that shows on the (obsolescent) fathoms charts and the new metric charts. Since the use of lights seen just rising or dipping is so useful, a clear understanding of this difference is important.

On fathoms charts the distance in miles, eg. *Beachy Head, 103 ft. 16 M*, 16 M is the distance in miles at which this light would rise if the observer's height of eye were 15 ft. This the geographical range only for 15 ft height of eye. If your height of eye were less than 15 ft, say 6 ft, the rising distance for you would be 1·7 M less, i.e. say $14\frac{1}{2}$ M.

On a metric chart we should find *Beachy Head 31 m. 25 M*. 25 M is called the nominal range, which is the luminous range when met: visibility is 10 M. It is based on the intensity of the light only, and takes no account of the elevation of the light, the observer's height of eye, nor of the limitations imposed by the curvature of the earth. It is the distance it is visible, provided one is high enough to see it over the horizon. To find Beachy Head's rising distance we must use its listed height (called *elevation*)—in this case 31 m, and our own height of eye, and consult the table of lights seen just rising or dipping. Elevation 31 m and height of eye 10 ft gives a vast difference from the nominal 25 M given on the chart.

If the (nominal) range given on the chart is small, say 5 M, it may well be that its geographical range

based on its height of say 5 m, is 8·1 M. In this case it is useless for determining our distance off when we first see it. Its intensity (brightness) is such that no matter how great our height of eye, we probably could not see it further than about 5 M.

Position by line of soundings
Whenever closing the land, if there is any doubt at all as to the yacht's position due to darkness or poor visibility, frequent soundings should be taken and compared with the charted depth at the estimated position. If, after correction of depth for the approximate height of tide, the two do not correspond, the EP must be suspect.

A series of soundings taken at regular intervals (a 'line of soundings') can, in suitable places, give a good guide to the yacht's position. A convenient interval between sounding might be between one and two miles apart. The intervals can be either time intervals, e.g. every 15, or 30 minutes, or distances sailed, e.g. every two miles by the log. The former is simpler if any tidal stream is running. Tidal stream must be dealt with since we must know the direction of the yacht's track over the ground. An example will clarify:

A yacht takes a series of echo sounder readings. After correction for height of tide, the soundings to be compared with the chart are:

Time	Log reading	Distance between soundings	Sounding
0415	84.0	2.5	15 m.
0445	86.5	2.5	14 m.
0515	89.0	2.5	14 m.
0545	91.5	2.5	21 m.
0615	94.0	2.5	17 m.
0645	96.5	2.5	28 m.

Course steered 085°T. Stream setting 240° at 1 kn throughout.

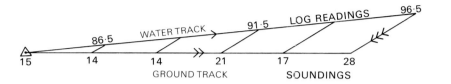

Fig 87. Position by soundings. Recorded soundings are plotted and the current allowed for.

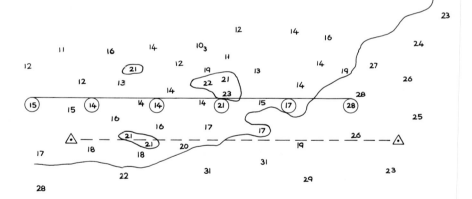

Fig 88 Position line by soundings. With the aid of tracing paper the line of soundings is moved on the chart to see if it fits.

Procedure

Make a water track/tidal stream/track vector, either on the chart, or on plain paper to the chart scale.

Along the water track line mark off the intervals between the soundings. From each sounding point on the water track lay off lines parallel to the tidal stream line to cut the track line. (Fig 87.)

Mark the soundings along the track line, and determine the direction of the track (091°T).

Place the edge of a piece of paper (or transparent paper) along the track line and write the soundings at the track line intervals along the paper edge.

Place the paper edge on the chart, exactly parallel to the direction of the track (091°T), the first sounding figure being placed near the EP at the time of the first sounding.

Check if all the soundings on the paper edge correspond closely with the charted soundings. If they do not correspond, slide the paper around keeping it parallel to the track line direction, till the position of best fit of actual soundings to chart soundings is found. The position of the last sounding should be the yacht's position when this sounding was taken.

Finally, slide the paper around (still parallel to the track line direction) to check whether a close match can be found anywhere else in the vicinity. If such a place is found, doubt exists and further soundings must be taken and the process repeated, or the new EP treated with great caution. (Fig 88.)

Composite fixes

There is thus a wide variety of methods of determining position lines and circles of position, any two or more being used together to provide a fix. There is no reason why a position line (or circle) obtained by one means should not be combined with another obtained by a different means. Combinations might be:

A distance off by vertical sextant angle or by rising or dipping distance with a single compass bearing.

A position circle by horizontal sextant angle of two objects with a compass bearing of only one.

A line of soundings and a DF radio bearing.

A transit of two objects and a distance off by VSA.

Where two (or more) methods are available in a given situation, chose those which are likely to be the most accurate. And remember these points:

The most accurate fix is one obtained visually.

The closer the observed object is to the yacht the more accurate will be the position found.

Position lines should 'cut' at a good wide angle, that is between about 50° and 120°.

If three objects (suitably positioned) can be identified, horizontal sextant angles will give the most accurate fix.

Whenever possible, obtain three position lines.

The size of the 'cocked hat' gives a good indication of the accuracy of each PL.

Do not use any object unless you can positively identify it both visually and on the chart.

When within soundings, check the depth (corrected to CD) with that shown on the chart at the 'fix' found. If they do not correspond closely, the fix is suspect and all bearings and workings should be checked.

Check and re-check the characteristics of lights before using, to guarantee correct identification.

Mark the fix and note against it the time and date, and write against each PL its bearing (or range) so that this can be checked.

Position finding by radio systems is explained in the next chapter. Position lines so found may of course also be combined with any found by visual means or by soundings.

10. Electronic position finding

Position finding at sea by electronic means is now relatively simple in small craft and the position can be read off instantly at the chart table. As has already been inferred, it is no exaggeration to say that this has transformed yacht navigation. Subject to failure from various causes (which can never be ruled out), many, perhaps, even most, of the well developed ways of finding where you are in small craft and deciding how best to get to the next destination are redundant. All the time navigational equipment is becoming smaller, relatively cheaper, more reliable and taking less current (from a 12 V or other low voltage system). More and more facilities are offered, more calculations are instantly worked out, more alarms are sounded, or corrections automatically made.

There is just no comparison with even terrestrial aids of long standing. Take the lighthouse. The crew says that a light has been sighted. The navigator gets hold of the hand bearing compass, opens the hatch and stares into the rain. For two minutes he checks the light with the stop watch, decides on its period and characteristic. Then he takes a bearing, the compass jumping about in the seaway. It is never still, but experience gives him a mean bearing. Then below again to drip water over the chart, identify the mark and plot a position line.

Even using a marine radio beacon, life is not much easier, though the work can all be done below. Tune into the frequency (this may be pre-set on modern receivers) and wait for the morse identification (or check against programmed time in the cycle). Then the bearing must be found in the one limited minute allowed for that beacon, which if missed may not return for six further minutes (unless it is continuous like some marine and all aeronautical ones). Is the null point exact? Not often! Once again experience helps as the navigator, earphones clamped on, interpolates the variable whistles and tones to find the null point. He will probably want to check it again in the next cycle.

By that time the yacht may have sailed almost a mile further. Then that too must be plotted. Neither of these operations have given a fix, only a position line, and a suitable (see Chapter 9) second position line must be found; one position line is liable to be more reliable than the other. Errors that can arise with a direction finding compass and ferrite rod picking up a marine radio beacon include coastal refraction, night effect and quadrantal error. There can also be misidentification of the station and incorrect reading of the compass (which usually has small figures on a small card).

Fig 89.   A summary of radio position finding systems.

RADIO POSITION FINDING SYSTEMS			
SYSTEM	**COVERAGE**	**METHOD**	**ACCURACY IN METRES**
SATNAV (TRANSIT)	WORLD-WIDE BUT NON-CONTINUOUS	DOPPLER SHIFT SATELLITE MEASURE	20 MINUTE DELAY THEN AVERAGE 1½ HOUR WAIT 500 + 500 per knot
OMEGA	WORLD-WIDE CONTINUOUS. SUBJECT TO INTERFERENCE	10-14 kHz HYPERBOLIC	DAY: 2000 NIGHT: 4000
LORAN-C (Groundwave)	NORTH AMERICA, NORTH OF UK, MEDITERRANEAN, NORTH PACIFIC CONTINUOUS	100 kHz HYPERBOLIC	70 at 50 mile range
LORAN-C (Skywave)	NORTHERN NORTH ATLANTIC, NORTHERN NORTH PACIFIC CONTINUOUS	100 kHz HYPERBOLIC	200
DECCA	EUROPE, NORTH CAPE TO GIBRALTAR AND SOME OTHER AREAS CONTINUOUS	80-120 kHz HYPERBOLIC	50 at 50 mile range
RADIO DIRECTION FINDING	WITHIN RANGE OF COASTAL STATION SUBJECT TO INTERFERENCE AND NIGHT ERROR	MEDIUM FREQUENCY INTERMITTENT TO PROGRAMME	VARIES PRACTICE NEEDED
GPS (Global positioning system)	WORLD-WIDE CONTINUOUS, BUT FROM ABOUT 1992	RANGE TO 3 OR MORE SATELLITES FROM CONFIGURATION OF 18	100 FOR CIVIL USE 16 FOR MILITARY

All this contrasts with merely reading off the latitude and longitude at the chart table and drawing two lines on the chart: they intersect the position. It is done. Or else the bearing and distance to the next mark (the waypoint) is read straight off. Touch the button and you have course and distance over the ground.

Available systems

A list of radio navigation systems is shown in Fig 89. Those of immediate interest for passage making are TRANSIT, Decca and Loran C. From the early nineties GPS will be introduced and will eventually provide a universal position finding system by land or sea anywhere in the world instantaneously.

Loran C is run by the U.S. Coast Guard. Its coverage and that of the other systems is shown in Admiralty List of Radio Signals, publication NP 285a. Roughly speaking, if you are anywhere on the eastern or western seaboards of the U.S.A. and Canada or in the Great Lakes, that is the system. It is universally used by U.S. yachtsmen. Other areas include Japan to the Philippines and the northern North Atlantic from the British Isles to Iceland and Greenland. Off the British Isles it is only effective when one is north of a line mid-Wales to the Wash and north of the south coast of Ireland. It operates in the Mediterranean, though not in the extreme east and west of that sea.

Decca is operated by the British company Racal Decca Marine. Roughly it works 250 miles offshore from the western coasts of Europe and the British Isles from North Cape to Gibraltar and just into the Mediterranean. (Fig 90). There are some Decca

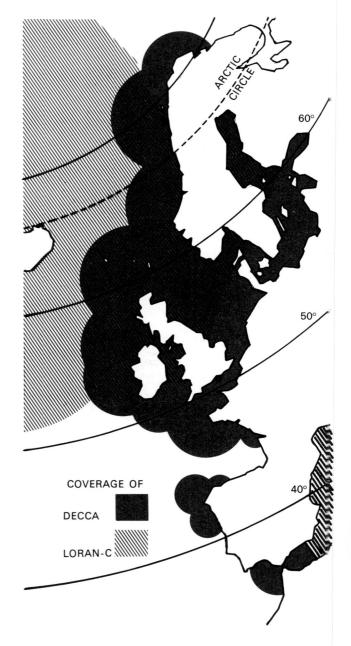

Fig 90. The area covered by Decca position finding off western Europe. This shows 24 hour accuracy, but greater areas are available by day only, completing the gaps in Biscay and off Portugal. Loran C coverage lies to the north of the British Isles.

areas elsewhere, such as the Gulf, South Africa and north-east Canada.

TRANSIT operates world wide covering all the areas in which Decca and Loran C are found, but the difference is that it is not continuous. Because there is a fix only when a satellite passes, there may be intervals of up to three hours between fixes. It is therefore primarily for ocean use, where Decca and Loran are out of range and precise position from minute to minute is less important.

There is another world-wide system called Omega, which is maintained by eight landbased transmitters with base lines between them of up to 5000 miles long. Natural phenomenon can interrupt Omega, notably ionospheric disturbance and polar cap absorption. The navigator has to know within four nautical miles his position, otherwise it is not possible to find the correct lane. Therefore once the Omega set is operating it has to be left switched on (this also applies to some extent to other systems). Decca, Loran C and Omega all come under the definition of hyperbolic aids.

Decca

Decca is the favoured system for continuous position finding and associated facilities around the British Isles and the west coasts of Europe. Chains of transmitting stations are established in the areas on shore. A typical chain consists of a master and two slave stations located between 60 and 120 miles from the master. The transmitters use different frequencies which relate to a basic frequency. The frequency differences enable the position to be identified by zones, slave station 'colours' and lanes or fractions of lanes. Sets for yachts (for instance Decca Yacht Navigator Marks III and IV) give a

practical yacht navigator

latitude/longitude read out at all times. The possible
error is 50 metres at 50 miles from the station and
200 metres at 200 miles from the station.

The Decca is usually set up in harbour before
starting the passage. The approximate latitude and
longitude are fed in and the set then searches and
calculates the exact position. The set can be left on
(using less than 0.2 amperes), or switched off when
its battery operated memory then will keep the
readings. It must however be switched on before the
yacht moves its position otherwise it will lose its
way. Up to twenty-five waypoints can be fed in
before leaving harbour and a sail plan set up. The
exact clock time and date are entered and these are
retained indefinitely by the memory without any
power being on.

Out of these entries, once you are sailing in or out
of sight of land, by compass or to windward, in fog
or clear weather, in near calm or severe gale, the
following facilities are instantly available. *Position* to
one hundredth of a minute (= 20 metres, but this is
the reading not the accuracy, which is mentioned
above). *Course and speed* over the ground for a
selected period (e.g. 2 minutes, 10 minutes):
compare this with course and speed through the
water as given by compass and boat speed read out.
Course and distance to waypoint and the estimated
time of arrival at it. *Distance off track* between
waypoints. The sequence of waypoints (*sail plan*).
Man overboard function for instant position
recording. *Fuel* monitor. Information as to what
Decca chain is being used. Built in *lighting. Date,
time, alarm clock* and *stop watch*.

There are audible alarms for a number of
occurrences such as low battery voltage, antenna
failure, waypoint approach, low speed, position
uncertainty (by calculation of the set), but these can
be entered by the user and are under his control
quantitively (e.g. the low voltage can be entered at
a chosen figure, say 10 volts or 10.8 volts). A cockpit

Decca Navigator Mark III for immediate position fixing up to 250
miles off western European shore. Provides numerous other
calculated information. The smaller display is a watertight cockpit
repeater.

repeater will show any reading, but is particularly useful for course and distance to the next waypoint.

Waypoint navigation

A waypoint is the latitude and longitude of the point of change from one track to the next (Fig 91). It may be an actual mark such as a buoy or a selected point on the chart, perhaps the corner of a shoal. It may also be a final destination, or an intermediate point along a theoretical straight track.

For a given passage use the chart(s) to make a list of waypoint lat/longs; then enter them in the Decca (or other set). Each waypoint has a number and a note must be kept by the navigator of name or easily referred position against waypoint number. On the display waypoint 1 is shown as PO1 in this case. Once all the waypoints are in, the sail plan is put in order and 'sail plan auto on'. As the yacht passes each waypoint, bisecting the angle between the courses, a new waypoint reading will appear giving the way to the next waypoint. The sail plan can be 'edited' at any time to vary the order, or jump a waypoint.

There are advantages over simply plotting lat/long positions on the chart, one being, that with discretion, the chart need not be consulted, but the waypoint homed on, possibly direct from a cockpit repeater. At all times the Decca can be switched rapidly between lat/long, bearing and distance to waypoint and present course and speed. As mentioned, an alarm can be set as a waypoint is neared: this will prevent you hitting it, if it is solid! Waypoints are not only used with Decca, but also with Loran C and TRANSIT.

Loran C

Loran C gives the same results as Decca. It also has a chain, though of from three to five stations spaced

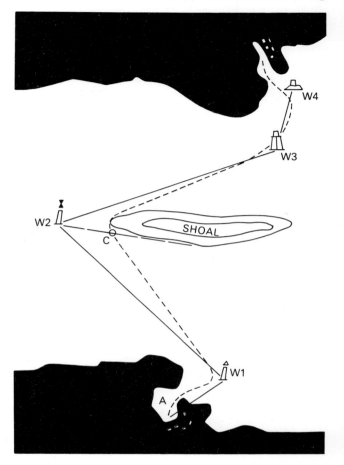

Fig 91. Waypoint navigation using Decca or Loran C. Waypoint 0 is set in harbour A; then W1, W2, W3 and W4 are fed into the set's 'sail plan'. W0 to W1 crosses land, so obviously actual track is not followed. When yacht reaches C and cuts corner, Decca changes waypoint on bisection of change of courses (also sounds alarm). Thereafter she closes with track at W3 and W4 and enters harbour B, in this case, by conventional navigation.

between several hundred miles apart with a master and at least two secondaries. They transmit on the same frequency, 100 kHz, but vary the time of pulses which the receiver identifies to find its position. The accuracy is about 70 m close to transmitters and around 200 m at the centre of a group coverage. Unlike Decca, Loran C has skywaves, which means it is effective over far greater distances, but sometimes these lack accuracy, though the set should warn of this. In the less well provided areas, it is essential for the Loran set to have a notching filter to cut out noise and this is particularly the case around the British Isles, where Decca can interfere with Loran C. There is a far greater range of available sets for Loran than Decca, the reasons being that Loran is not a 'private' network and the large markets and mass manufacturers in the U.S.A. and Japan are at work. A simple 'cheap' set which may be satisfactory off the U.S. seaboard where signals are strong, may not do for northern Europe, where noise ratio is high and the required notching has to be applied for the set to be fully sensitive to the exact frequency. In the U.S. the frequency is compulsorily kept clear, but in Europe there is various interference; even Prague radio has been known to upset Loran C reception in the Mediterranean. By the way, Loran A was a former, less accurate system and has now been phased out.

Walker Satnav 412 for position fixing by TRANSIT system. It needs additional dead reckoning information owing to length of time between fixes.

SATNAV (TRANSIT)

TRANSIT is worldwide and supplied by five orbiting satellites, yet, as already mentioned not continuous. The satellites are at a height of 1073 kilometres and form a kind of birdcage arround the earth, each satellite circuiting the earth in 107 minutes. In outline the yacht receiver gets its position from the doppler effect. A 400 MHz frequency is used and the receiver counts the frequency difference due to the motion of the satellite. The receiver re-calculates an assumed DR position, maybe doing this several times. The display therefore shows the position as it was at a time specified on the set. It is out of date straight away and so more dead reckoning data must be fed into the TRANSIT set in the yacht. As this depends on estimated tidal set and similar variables the limitation of TRANSIT in coastal waters can be understood. The interval may be as long as eighteen minutes. It is therefore of considerable advantage for TRANSIT to be interfaced with log reading and an eletronic compass (such as the Brookes and Gatehouse Halcyon 2). A yacht crossing the Atlantic from Europe to the U.S.A. might well have TRANSIT for the ocean and Loran C for instantaneous position finding when coastal waters are reached.

GPS (Global Positioning System)

In the early 1990's will come GPS.
Instantaneous position will be obtainable from
satellite, because eighteen will be orbiting to give
complete global coverage and there will always be
one or more giving the yacht receiver its position.
The accuracy may be half a cable for civilian use
(100 metres), but less (16 metres) for military use.
GPS is run by the U.S. Defence Department and is
the most likely for universal use, though Europe is
developing NAVSAT and the USSR is developing
GLONASS for the same purpose.

Once GPS, or its equivalent, is established,
sets will become relatively cheap since they will be
used by everyone everywhere on land (expeditions,
surveyors etc.) and on sea as well as in the air.
Probably Decca and Loran will no longer be
necessary and GPS sets will be built in to all yachts
and integrated to give instant navigational data of
any conceivable type.

11. Radar for Some

The vast majority of commercial vessels are now equipped with radar, and every year more compact and cheaper sets are produced, for use on yachts both sail and power. Radar now constitutes a valuable aid to navigation. Radar *is* only an aid, and does not replace the traditional methods and practices of navigation. The human eye is a wonderful instrument, provided visibility is suitable. But when visibility is restricted it is then that any additional aid to navigation is welcome. Radar is such an aid, but it has certain distinct limitations and problems in its interpretation which it is essential are well appreciated if the radar set is not to be a danger rather than a help. As is well known, collisions and strandings of ships fitted with radar and with qualified watchkeeping officers on the bridge still occur, which emphasizes the importance of a knowledge of radar's capabilities and limitations.

Radar equipment

Radar equipment for a yacht consists of:
1. A generator or alternator,
2. A transceiver,
3. A scanner,
4. A display unit.

The generator or alternator converts the ship's electrical supply of any voltage between 12 v and 220 v to that required for the radar. Power consumption varies between 75 watts and about 240 watts, depending on the model.

The transceiver generates and controls outgoing electrical impulses which are radio waves of extremely short wavelength (3–5 cm) which, like light waves, travel in a straight line. The transceiver also receives and processes the returning incoming echos reflected back from any object struck, or 'target'. It is connected by a special lead called a 'waveguide' to the scanner.

This is a form of aerial designed to project the outgoing signals in a narrow beam or 'lobe', and also to collect the returning echos for passing back to the transceiver. The scanner rotates, so that the beam sweeps round, rather as does the light of a lighthouse.

The display unit, or plan position indicator (PPI) contains a cathode ray tube, the flat surface of which is 20 cm in diameter. As in a TV tube, the inner surface is coated with material which glows on the impact of electrons and displays the relative position of targets from which echos of radar waves are received back. All controls are located on, or close to, the display unit.

The scanner is a horizontal arm, vertically pivoted, rotated by power at (usually) 25 r.p.m. in a horizontal plane. On some sets the rotating scanner is enclosed in a plastic 'Radome' so that halyards and sheets cannot become entangled. A scanner not in a radome must be carefully sited where it is safely clear of any obstruction. The scanner weighs between 14–23 kg, and must be installed as high as possible and where there will be the minimum of obstruction to its 'seeing' all round. On a power yacht, it may be mounted on a small plinth on coachroof or wheelhouse roof, or on a short mast. The plane of rotation should be horizontal when the yacht is under way. In planing power boats, this may require it to point downwards and ahead when the vessel is at rest or off the plane. In sailing craft the preferred position is well up the forward side of the mizzenmast. The scanner should not be sited where persons would normally be in its immediate 'line of fire' (e.g. level with bridge or cockpit) as some radiation is emmited. It should be not less than 2 m from the compass.

The display unit or PPI is positioned convenient to the helmsman but at least 1 m from the steering compass. The transceiver may be sited anywhere convenient. Some makes incorporate it with the scanner unit: others with the display unit.

Radar principles

An echo sounder works on the principle of measuring the time taken for an impulse sent out from the yacht to be reflected back from the sea bed, and received. Radar works on the same principle, but measures not only the time taken for an impulse to be reflected back from an object in its path, but is also able to show the direction of the object from the transmitter. Thus the radar can show both distance away, and bearing, of a target.

To visualize the action, consider first what happens if the scanner is not rotating. At the instant that a pulse is sent out from the scanner, an electron is 'fired' by the cathode ray tube at the centre of the tube's display face, and a tiny beam of electrons is directed outward towards the circumference, arriving at the time required for an echo received from an object (if any) at the distance (or range) for which the controls have been set. The train of electrons forms a line on the screen as the surface retains the glow for a split second (as on a TV screen). The length of the line is known as the time base.

When the pulse has bounced back from any object in its path it is picked up by the scanner, processed and fed into the cathode ray tube where it causes a bright spot on the time base line, the distance out from the centre being exactly proportional to the target's distance from the ship. The time base line is suppressed so that only the returning impulse shows up. The range so established can be extremely accurate.

When the scanner is revolving at a set speed, the time base line (not visible) rotates around the centre of the screen at the same speed, crossing the 'heading line' (or lubberline) when the scanner is 'looking' directly ahead. In this way the bearing of any reflected impulse is shown on the screen, relative to ship's head, which is shown on the screen as a steady thin line from the centre to the forward edge, the heading line. Most sets have a bearing cursor, a line engraved on a transparent disc over the screen, the line running from the centre to the circumference. By turning a knob, the cursor can be rotated so that the line cuts any target's trace and the end of the cursor line indicates its relative bearing on a 360° scale around the screen. Some sets are marked 0° round to 360°: others are marked 0° to 180°, to left and right.

Radar displays, like charts, are scaled. A large scale chart shows a small area in great detail; a small scale chart shows a larger area but in less detail, distances on land or sea being represented by smaller distances on the chart. Radar sets can

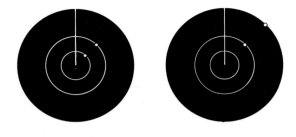

Fig 92.   Different ranges set on PPI. Left hand at 12 miles, right at 6 miles. Targets in each case north east 3 miles and 6 miles.

in length, so that both bearing and range can be read at once. Indication of range (or distance away) is extremely accurate, and more reliable than the indication of bearing.

Various other controls are fitted, for tuning the transmitting and receiving units in harmony, for reducing 'clutter' caused by signals being received back from wave crests, for varying the brightness or contrast, and so on. These all have vital parts to play and it is essential to master the maker's instructions in their purpose and use.

The shape of the beam of radar pulses sent out is of interest. The horizontal axis is kept as narrow as possible to give clear bearing direction, and is about 2° wide. The vertical axis is much wider—about 25°—to allow for rolling and

Fig 93.   Width of vertical axis of radar pulse, necessary because of movement of ship, gives rise to false echos.

be adjusted to various 'scales', in discreet steps. The more usual scales, or 'ranges', are 1½, 3, 6, 12, over 12 nautical miles. (Fig 92.) When switched to the 12-mile range, the distance represented from the centre to the edge of the screen is 12 miles. A target trace appearing half-way out would indicate a target 6 miles away. Another trace a quarter the way out from the centre, 3 miles away. If the set were switched to the 6-mile range, the first trace at 6 miles range would jump to the edge of the screen and the second one to the half-way distance. To enable the range of a target to be gauged, 'range rings' are projected on to the screen, their circumference being at set distances from the centre. Interpolation of the range of targets falling between two rings is simple. Some sets have a variable range indicator, a circle of light which can be manually adjusted so that it touches the inner edge of the target. The range is then read from the adjusting control. Another version is the 'Interscan' fitted to some radar sets. This is an electronic bearing cursor which can be adjusted

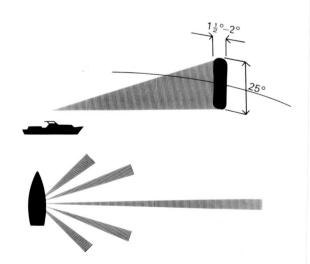

pitching of the vessel on which the radar is carried. It is not possible to confine all pulses to the main beam: some escape out at an angle, forming side 'lobes', which can give rise to additional, false echoes at short range. (Fig 93.)

In clear weather the range at which one can see an object is governed by the observer's height of eye and the height of the object, because light travels in a straight line. Radar beams also travel in a straight line because of their extremely short wavelength. In Fig 94 the high ground B will be shown on the radar screen, but not A. As the yacht nears the coast, A will start reflecting some pulses and its trace also will appear in the screen.

The screen is coated inside with material which glows as the electrons strike it, thus producing the trace of the target. This spot continues to glow (diminishing in brightness) until after the time base line has swept over it again. A stationary target seen from a stationary operating ship will appear as a stationary spot on trace. But if ship and target are moving relative to each other, that is, either or both are moving, each successive sweep will show the trace in a slightly different position, but the 'afterglow' of the previous positions will show up, giving the trace a 'tail'. This tail must not be confused with the shape or 'aspect' of the target.

It is important to remember that positions, and movements, of targets seen on the screen are all relative to the operating ship's position, which is always at the centre of the screen. All stationary objects (buoys, the land) will appear to move in the opposite direction to that of the operating ship, and their tails will show this. (Fig 95.)

The appearance of a trace on the PPI gives some indication of its character as follows (Fig 96.):

Breakwaters and piers make good targets, reflect well and show up clearly on the PPI.

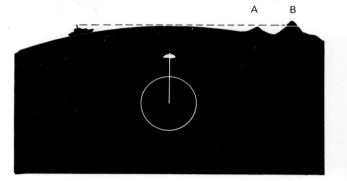

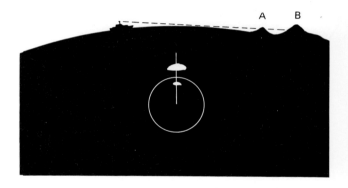

Fig 94.   Due to earth's curvature, ship does not at first see high ground A: first sighting shows only B. Later coastal high ground A appears on the tube.

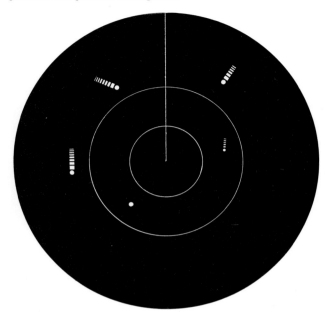

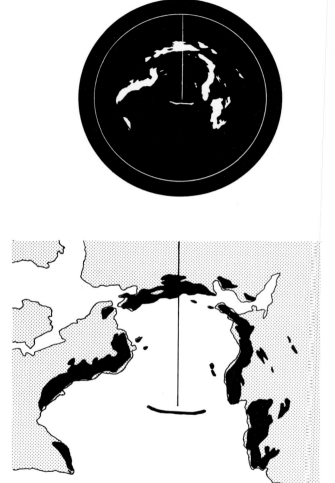

Fig 95.   What you see on the PPI tube. 'Tails' indicate (top right) ship on collision course, but not necessarily bows on to observer; then moving round clockwise, buoy which you are sailing past; ship on same course and speed (no tail); ship on reciprocal course; ship which will pass ahead, if it maintains course and speed.

Fig 96.   Typical display on PPI (Plymouth Sound). Lower chart shows location of high ground and floating objects (ships, buoys with radar reflectors) which the radar has picked up.

Lighthouses do not show up so well as their tubular shape diffuses the signal.

Rocky and steep hills reflect well, but shallow hills with vegetation produce a weak 'paint' on the PPI.

Low beaches, reefs or sandbanks will only be indicated when within the horizon distance for the height of the scanner, and may be obscured by sea clutter.

The shape or 'aspect' of another vessel can seldom be determined until she is within 2 miles, or further in the case of large tankers and other big vessels.

Buoys and radar beacons

A metal navigational buoy will show up on the PPI as a small trace. If it is fitted with a radar reflector, at greater range and more brightly. When in any doubt as to the name (and hence the position) of a buoy observed on the PPI, sail up to it and (by day) read the name painted on it. Some buoys are specially equipped so that they can be identified by the trace on the PPI. These are:

(a) The Racon. Marked on the chart surrounded by a magenta ring and the word 'Racon' beside. An increasing number of light vessels and lighthouses, and some important buoys are so fitted. The Racon is an omnidirectional radar transmitter which is triggered off when it receives a pulse from a ship's radar.

This causes the trace on the ship's PPI to be in the form of a bar or bold line, directed to the ship's position (centre of PPI) the nearer end representing the position of the Racon. The range a racon will show up is the radar horizon of the ship's set. At present there are few of these in use.

(b) The Ramark. Marked on the chart surrounded by a magenta ring and the word 'Ramark' beside it. The trace appears as a bar of light (similar to

Raytheon light weight radar mounted on a motor cruiser.

Light float (in Liverpool Bay) moored at its 'bow' where vertical stripes indicate mid-Channel mark. In a frame on the top of this, there is a racon device.

the Racon) but with a given number of 'breaks' in it. However it gives an independent transmission and does not need the ship's radar to trigger it off.

Navigation by radar

When making a landfall with radar in operation, all the usual preparations should be made. A large scale chart should be marked with the yacht's EP, offlying dangers searched for on the chart, depths checked and compared with soundings. Objects likely to be first observed by radar should be found on the chart. This will involve examining the charted heights and approximate bearings and range of high ground, as these will be the first to come up on the PPI.

If observations are started in good time while some miles off, the shore line is most unlikely to show up, but separate traces of the peaks of high ground may appear. These should be plotted on transparent paper or on a large Douglas protractor, laying off their relative bearings, and ranges to the same scale as the chart. If three or more 'peaks' can be so plotted, the yacht's position can be found by moving the paper or protractor around on the chart till each object marked coincides with a hill of comparable height on the chart. Range is likely to be more accurate than bearing, so when a probable 'fix' has been found, check it by using the range on the set as a radius and drawing circular arcs.

All arcs should intersect at a single

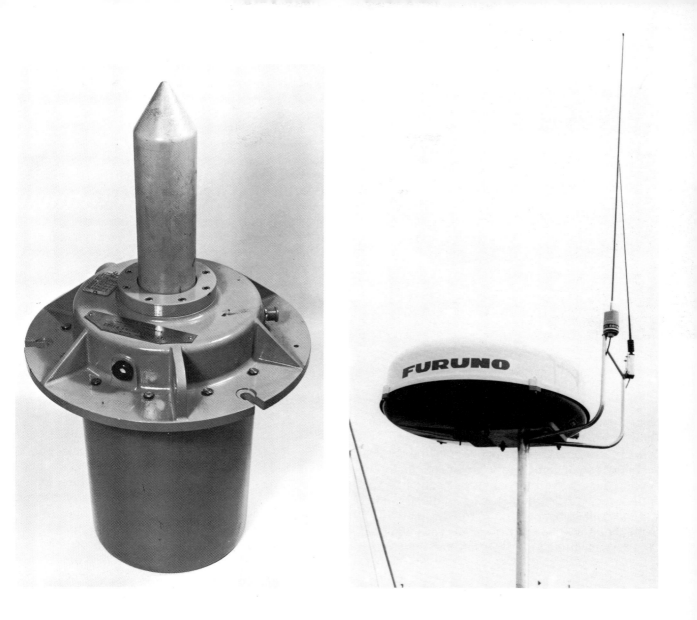

Racon device: fitted to a navigational mark this emits a signal which is triggered by a radar set and is identifiable on a radar tube.

On sailing boats the siting of radomes is not so straightforward; here a special mounting has been made clear of sails and spars on *Quailo*, ex. *Crusade*.

Radar display unit of small size. This EMI Electrascan weighs 33 lb and measures 9½ in. × 12 in. × 19½ in. and can run on a 12 volt supply.

to true heading if the bearing is to the right of the heading marker; subtract if to the left.

A low shore line will not show up at any great distance, and it is important to study the height of the land near the coast. (Fig 97.)

Reliable bearings of other ships or landmarks and buoys can *only* be obtained when own ship is steering a *steady course*. If the yacht is allowed to yaw all targets will appear to move round radially.

When taking action to avoid a collision, *or* to prevent a close quarters situation developing, take action in *good time*, and make a *bold* alteration of course or speed. A 90° course alteration, or more, is none too much.

A valuable use of radar is the avoidance of collision. While correct use will enable the presence of another vessel to be detected while some miles off, it is equally important to be visible to the other vessel. For this reason a radar reflector is strongly recommended, particularly for a yacht built of wood or GRP. One model

point if the objects have been correctly identified.

All bearings taken from the PPI will be relative bearings. To convert these to true bearings for plotting, first convert the compass heading to true in the usual way. If the PPI is calibrated 0°–360°, add the relative bearing to the true heading (subtracting 360° if the answer exceeds 360°). If the PPI is calibrated 0°–180° left and right, add it

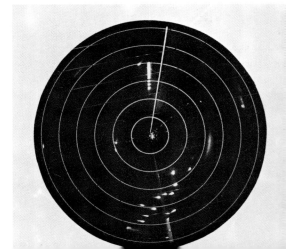

Radar tube including a view of the racon signal in morse, close to the mark with its normal tail.

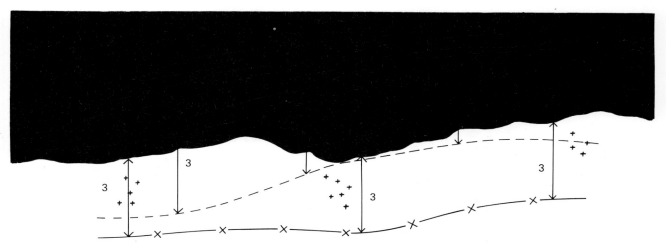

Fig 97. Using radar for distance off. The navigator wants to stay 3 miles off the shore (solid track with crosses). His mistake would be to stay 3 miles from hills showing on radar tube. Then he would be on dangerous (pecked line) course.

(Electroscan, by EMI Marine) incorporates an automatic alarm which, when set, gives audible warning of any target (ship, coast, rocks) appearing on the PPI.

Correct *interpretation* of what is shown on the PPI is essential for avoiding collisions. In visual navigation we have the benefit of usually knowing the 'aspect' of an approaching vessel, of seeing which way she is heading. This is not the case with radar, until the vessel is getting close. However, radar can be used to indicate whether the other vessel's relative bearing is steady or changing, by lining up the cursor line over her trace and observing whether it stays on this line. If it does, or if it does not move distinctly away

Ordinary radar reflector on a navigational buoy. Do not confuse with characteristic top mark.

clear weather and checking the images seen on the PPI with visual observations. The wheel can be turned over to a competent helmsman and courses determined from PPI information given him. This soon shows up the competence of the radar operator.

A summary on radar for yachts

Radar on a yacht is a valuable aid, but only an aid, to navigation. All other methods of establishing the yacht's position and track which the circumstances permit being used, should still be employed. In particular, the yacht's EP should be able to be plotted at any required time by the usual methods of recording courses steered, distances run, tidal streams, etc.

Practice at sea, following thorough study, is essential.

Practice in clear weather by day, when the PPI display can be compared with what is seen visually, is most valuable.

Objects below the horizon (as viewed from the scanner) will not be shown on the PPI.

The radar set must be checked, and kept in tune, strictly as laid down in the maker's instructions.

An object behind a higher or larger one may not be shown, such as an estuary behind a headland.

Two or more small objects close together may appear as a single object.

Low targets may be lost in sea clutter or heavy rain.

A small object may not show up at extremely short range.

Range is more accurately given than bearing.

from this line, the vessels are on a collision course, or 'risk of collision exists'. The action to be taken, and methods of checking its effectiveness and of plotting are beyond the scope of this book, but should be thoroughly mastered. It should be noted that the International Regulations for Preventing Collisions at Sea (IRPCS) state that radar equipment if fitted and operational *shall* be used to determine whether a risk of collision exists. In restricted visibility a proper radar watch must be maintained.

Excellent practice in the use and interpretation of the radar set can be got by sailing in bright

12. Sailing to Windward

'If I was a gent sir, which I ain't sir, I wouldn't never sail to wind'ard, sir'.—paid hand in the days of gaff rig.

Nevertheless, there are plenty of occasions when the course to destination, or to the next point to be rounded, is to windward, and the direct course cannot be laid. The yacht must be sailed hard on the wind and tacked at intervals. The questions that then arise are:

(a) Should the first tack be on starboard or on port tack?
(b) How far should she sail on each successive tack, or when should she change tacks?

There is no simple answer to either question, which will depend on many factors including:

(a) The direction of the tidal stream at various times during the passage.
(b) The likelihood of the wind shifting during the passage, either by veering (changing direction clockwise), or backing (changing anti-clockwise).

These are the navigational hints for windward sailing (Fig 98.):

(a) On the chart, draw in the 'windward line'—a line back from the destination, in the direction of the true wind.

(b) Set 'tack limiting' lines on each side of the 'windward line', between which the yacht's track is to be kept.
(c) Other things being equal, sail on that tack which makes the smaller angle to the direction of the stream, or sail to place the stream on the yacht's lee bow in preference to the weather bow.
(d) Plot the yacht's progress, allowing for stream and leeway, so that an accurate track over the ground is recorded on the chart.
(e) Be prepared to re-assess the situation when wind direction or tidal stream alters.

Windward line

The direction of the 'true' wind can only be accurately determined by either:

(a) Observing the yacht's head by compass when she passes through the eye of the wind when tacking, or
(b) Observing the yacht's heading when close hauled first on one tack and then on the other, and deducing the mean between the two headings; e.g. starboard tack, 186° C, port tack 280° C, mean 233° C (convert to true for laying off on the chart).

When sailing on a tack the direction of the wind felt on board, the apparent wind, will be different from that of the true wind, which is the

direction you need to know. Apparent wind is
discussed later. A 'windward line' is laid off from
the destination (or turning point) back in the
direction of the true wind.

Tack limiting line

When sea room permits, it is possible to reach a
windward position in two long tacks, sailing on
one tack till a position is reached from which the
destination can be laid on the other track. (Fig 99.)
If this would result in the yacht sailing a long way
from the 'windward line', this is not to be
recommended because a change in wind direction
may result in her overstanding her destination,
i.e. on the second tack the wind may become so
free that she could have tacked much earlier, and
saved many hours sailing. (Fig 100.) Hence the
general rule not to sail too far away from the
windward line.

This is best insured by drawing tack limiting
lines on the chart. There are alternative ways of
doing this. First, draw in the windward line, or
line from destination back towards departure
point, in the direction of the true wind. Lay a
course to cross this 'windward line'. Once this
'windward line' is reached, successive tacks will
be made across this line. If no material change in
wind direction can be predicted, tack limiting
lines can be laid on each side of the windward
line. These may be:
(a) Lines parallel to and on each side of the
'windward line', spaced perhaps 10 miles apart
(the longer the passage the wider they may be).
(Fig 101.)
or (b) Lines drawn radiating FROM destination,
and making an angle of say 5° from the
'windward line', on each side of it. (Fig 102.)
or (c) A combination of both (a) and (b) say
parallel lines 10 miles apart till nearing destination,
when (say) 20° arc from destination is reached.

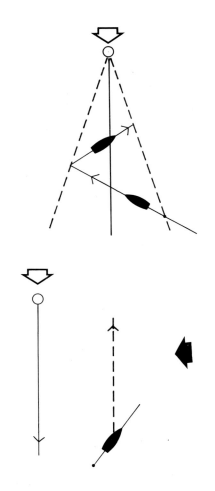

Fig 98.   General plans for windward sailing. Keep within tack
limiting lines and do not get 'far out' and so be caught to
leeward of destination by wind shift. But (lower picture) if
there is a cross tide, lee bow it until tide changes.

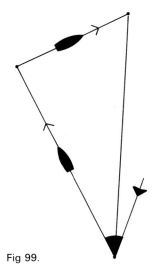

Fig 99.

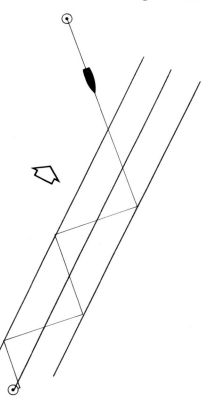

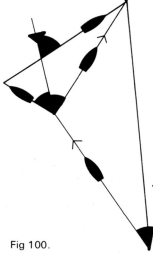

Fig 100.

Fig 101. Tack limiting lines about ten miles apart, but width depends on length of voyage.

Fig 99. This yacht on starboard tack simply holds it until she can lay the destination on port. The first leg may be one mile or one hundred and is all right if the wind direction remains steady.

Fig 100 More likely is a wind shift. In this case it backs. Red yacht sails on and has to sail further, black yacht tacks and fetches mark more easily than in Fig 98 situation.

157

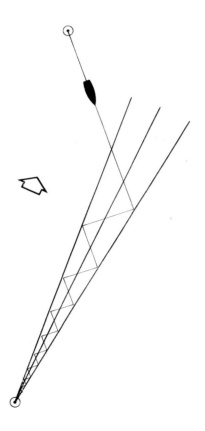

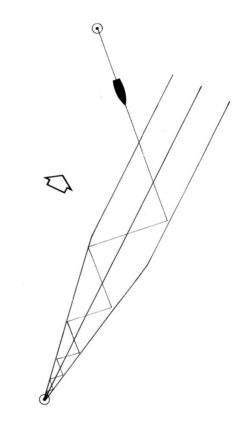

Fig 102   Tack limiting lines five degrees either side of line which is dead to leeward of destination.

Fig 103.   Combination of 100 and 101. As destination is neared, tacks become shorter.

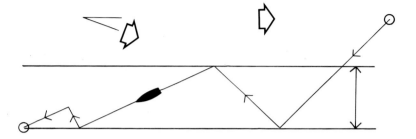

Fig 104. When the wind is expected to veer, draw the tack limiting lines on the right hand side of the destination. Note that yacht first sails into the planned limiting lines.

This produces a 'corridor' with parallel sides till it becomes prudent to shorten tacks progressively as the destination is neared. (Fig 103.)

If a windshift can be reasonably predicted (as when a cold front is forecast, which will probably be followed by the wind veering) then the tack limiting lines should be drawn on that side of the windward line towards which the wind is expected to change. (Fig 104.) This will ensure that when the windshift occurs the yacht will be on the then weather side of the original windward line, and can head up much closer to the destination.

An accurate record must be maintained of the yacht's track and the direction and speed she is making good over the ground should be calculated so that the time, and log reading, when she should reach the tack limiting line can be determined. The helmsman then knows when to tack again. Each time she tacks it is recommended that the direction of the true wind is checked, in case it has veered or backed.

When a substantial (and apparently established) change in wind direction occurs, a completely fresh appraisal should be made. The old windward line has lost all significance, the old tack limiting lines are obsolete and a fresh windward line and tack limiting lines should be drawn. If the wind has shifted as expected, the yacht should be well up to windward of her destination and (with luck) may be able to lay the direct course to the destination without further tacking. At worst, she will be able to make one long tack which will bring her much nearer the destination.

Tidal streams and lee-bow
One of the guide lines given earlier was to lee-bow the tidal stream when there is an option as to which tack to sail on. Fig 105 illustrates a yacht's track when lee-bowing the stream. In Fig 106 two yachts are shown. There are two

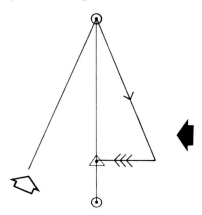

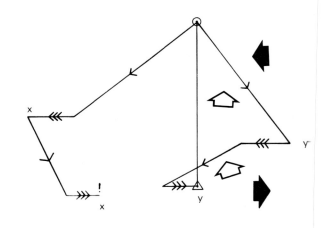

Fig 105.   Simple leebowing. Lucky yacht sails on starboard tack and gets lift to windward from west going stream to destination due south.

Fig 106.   The lee bow effect. There is much misunderstanding about the effect of lee bowing the tide. The proper application of the term concerns a cross tide where one tack would put the stream on the weather bow and the other tack would put the stream on the lee bow. As the lee bow tack is advantageous it follows that on a passage crossing several tides, it pays to tack when the stream changes. Here yacht Y is lee bowing the stream. Yacht X is sailing on a different tack and takes the tide on the weather bow. When the tide changes both yachts tack, but X is far from destination when Y gets there.

real advantages to be gained by 'lee-bowing' the stream when several tacks are involved:

(a) The lateral movement of the yacht, over the ground, caused by the stream, has the effect of altering the direction of the apparent wind in a favourable direction, allowing the yacht to sail closer to the true wind direction.
(b) There is also a slight improvement in the wind speed, which is particularly useful in light airs.

   To see how this comes about, consider a wind

vector, that is, a triangle whose sides are of lengths proportional to the wind speeds. First consider the conditions when there is no tidal stream.

Assume: Yacht's speed through the water   5 kr.
               True wind speed   10 kr.
               Yacht's heading, 45° off the true wind.
   The wind felt on deck (the 'apparent' wind) is the resultant of

(a) the true wind (10 kn)
(b) the yacht's own speed 5 kn. (Fig 107.)

If the yacht were motoring in flat calm, she would experience an 'apparent' wind from dead ahead, exactly equal to her own speed. This component is still present when she is experiencing a true wind, as in the the example.

From the wind vector we see that the yacht will experience an 'apparent' wind of 14 kn, coming from 30° from dead ahead. Now let us assume there is a stream flowing to the East at 2 kn, and no wind at all. If the yacht were drifting and making no way through the water, she would experience a wind of 2 kn blowing from the East towards the West. The stream has thus introduced a fresh wind component of 2 kn to westward. Let us draw the original wind vector but now omitting the true wind line, and adding the tidal stream wind line, 2 kn long, to westward. (Fig 108.) The new line 'apparent wind including stream effect' is 15·2 kn long, so the new 'apparent' wind's speed has increased from 14 to 15·2 kn, AND has swung round 7°. The wind has freed by 7° and if the yacht continues to sail 30° off the (new) 'apparent' wind she will be pointing 7° closer to windward.

There is no golden rule regarding the width apart of tacking limit lines—their purpose is simply to give guidance as to how far from the windward line it is wise to sail. Too far, and one may find a wind shift is expensive in time, too near and tacks are made too frequently. As we have seen, the tidal stream—if it will be setting across the course—will affect the direction of the apparent wind, and hence the course that can be made good to windward. There will be moments when it is better to disregard the precise position of a tack limiting line if by so doing a lee-bow effect can be continued for longer. Conversely, it may pay to tack before reaching a limit line if the stream is about to change.

When sailing to windward along a coast the

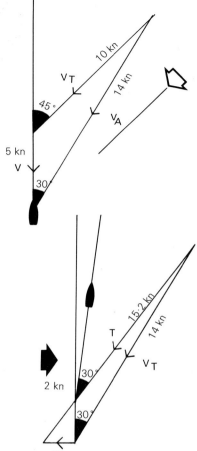

Fig 107. Apparent wind ($^V{}_A$ = 14 knots) is the resultant of true wind ($^V{}_T$ = 10 knots) and yacht speed (V = 5 knots).

Fig 108. Add a 2 knot stream (black solid arrow) to the apparent wind of Fig 106 and there is a further resultant wind (T = 15.2 knots). If the yacht is going to windward, she can also improve her heading as new wind has swung away from bows.

tidal streams may play a more predominating part in deciding tactics. Here it will pay to study the areas of the most favourable, and most unfavourable tidal streams. Clearly one would, when possible, tack so as to avoid areas of more unfavourable tide, and into areas of more favourable tide. In general, tides run strongest off headlands, weakest across bays, tend to set into and out of bays, change direction earlier close in, later further out. These points can be seen on tidal stream atlas or chart. The original track line drawn from departure to destination loses all significance when sailing to windward prevents this course being laid. The significant direction is that from the yacht's actual position at any time to destination (or intermediate turning point).

When ocean racing, careful and exact planning of the tactics to adopt when sailing a windward course are essential for success. But when cruising it is less important to be quite so painstaking. Nevertheless, the more thought put in, the sooner will the passage be completed, and if the going is rugged—as it may well be when sailing hard on the wind—any time that can be saved is usually very welcome.

13. Log Books

Written records of all happenings aboard a yacht are clearly essential for a number of purposes. For navigation, accurate details of courses steered, times and mileages, bearings taken and so on, are needed. Historical record, broader details of passages undertaken, times of departure and arrival, names of crew and similar details will be wanted. To attempt to incorporate all this in a single log book would be most cumbersome, and more than one record should be maintained, each for a specific purpose.

Every skipper and navigator has his own ideas as to what records should be maintained, and what details recorded. Some buy books already ruled up with columns headed for a variety of data. Others rule up their own book, constructed to record all, and only, the information they consider necessary. The records recommended are :
1. A *deck log*, in which the helmsman or person in charge of a watch, records all events as they occur.
2. A *navigator's log*, in which the navigator or skipper records only that data, extracted from the deck log, which is necessary to plot the yacht's position and progress.
3. A *ship's log*. This can be anything between a handsomely leather-bound book embossed with the yacht's name, and a hard-back note book. This gives the 'story' of each passage, listing the crew, details of departures and arrivals, interesting occurrences and so on. This can be written up by

the skipper daily, or at the end of a passage, from the information in the deck log, the navigator's log and from memory.
4. *Note book*. For recording all calculations.

The deck log
This will often be written up, or referred to, on deck, so a stout notebook (preferably of waterproof paper) is to be preferred. The ruling can be varied, but that recommended is shown. (Fig 109.) *Course required*. This is entered by the navigator *before* the watch takes over. It gives the course required to keep the yacht on the rhumbline to the destination (or to the next turning point). If the wind is free, then it is the actual course to be steered. If this course cannot be sailed because it would be too close to the wind, it indicates the course wanted if and when the wind permits, and the helmsman should not sail above this course should the wind come more abeam, without reference to the navigator.
Course steered. The helmsman enters this with the actual compass course he has been steering. With a free wind, this should be the same as 'Co reqd'. When sailing to windward the helmsman will be sailing as close to the wind as he can while maintaining a good speed, varying the course to accord with the wind by either watching his sails or (if fitted) the wind direction indicator. He must also watch his compass, and at the next deck log

DECK LOG *For Sailing Yacht*						
Date Time BST	*Log rdg:*	*Co. reqd.*	*Course steered since last entry*	*Wind*	*Baro.*	*Remarks*

Fig 109. Deck log for sailing yacht. This has essentials only.

entry time record his best estimate of the average or mean course steered since the last entry. The inexperienced helmsman should be cautioned of the importance of this being assessed as well as possible (and not over-optimistic).

Wind. The helmsman's assessment of the wind direction and strength, preferably in Beaufort notation (e.g. SW5). The skipper should make it a firm rule that at stated and regular intervals (say every half-hour) those on watch record all the items listed, and in the Remarks column if they occur, details of sail changes, tacks or gybes made, bearings taken or observations made of any landmarks. Even the sighting of steamers or other

DECK LOG *For Power Yacht*									
Date Time BST	*Log rdg:*	*Co. reqd.*	*Course steered since last entry*	*Wind*	*Baro.*	*Speed or RPM*	*Eng. temp.*	*Charge Amps*	*Remarks*

Fig 110. Deck log for power boat.

NAVIGATOR'S LOG												
Date Time BST	*Log Rgd:*	*Log Since last plot*	*Course C°*	*Course Dev: E+* W−*	*Course Var: E+* W−*	*T°*	*Lee Way P+* S−*	*Water Track T°*	*Stream Set °*	*Stream Rate kn*	*Stream Drft. Miles*	*Plot Ref. or Lat / Long.*
	** Signs operate when working → Reverse when working ←*											

Fig 111. Navigator's log extracts necessary information from deck log.

yachts may be not only of interest but of value to the navigator. The regular noting of the barometer can be of help in anticipating the onset of bad weather or a shift in the wind.

In a power yacht, the deck log (Fig 110.) should also record at reasonably frequent intervals details of the engine(s), such as r.p.m., temperature, oil pressure, ammeter. At perhaps less frequent intervals the state of fuel stocks should be recorded. The requirement to make these entries ensures that instruments are regularly read and any unusual change is observed. Even a small (but unaccountable) alteration in reading may give early warning of trouble brewing in the power house and enable the engineer/skipper to investigate it.

A small but useful tip. At the end of each day (at midnight) draw a line right across the page and below it, enter the new day and date. On a longish trip it is quite easy to use the wrong date (for tides, nautical almanac, etc).

Regular entry of the deck log is not only essential for navigation, but gives the man or men on watch an interest. They can check the speed, and if it drops off, check the trim of the sails (or the engine if under power). Both electronic and towed logs often get fouled by weed and either register slow, or stop. If the log is read every half-hour this is soon detected, the log cleared and the recorded mileage corrected.

The navigator's log

The object of this separate log (Fig 111.) is to record only that information, extracted from the deck log, which the navigator will need to plot the ship's progress and position. The navigator may decide to bring the chart up to date (i.e. plot the yacht's new position by DR or observations) every four hours, or at every change of watch, while on passage. As the destination, or any

dangers are neared, and depending on the visibility, he may plot at more frequent intervals.

An entry will be necessary at the time he wishes to make the next plot on the chart and on every alteration of course since the last entry, since each new course steered will require its own water track to be plotted. (Alternatively, the navigator may decide to calculate a new EP by Traverse Tables instead of by plotting, and for this he will need details of each course steered. See Chapter 17).

The Tidal Stream section entries will depend on circumstances. Streams seldom flow exactly as predicted, and interpolation between springs and neaps may be necessary, but very exact calculations are seldom called for. If the tidal atlas has been marked up in pencil with the times each chartlet applies on each day it is usually a simple matter to determine the average tidal stream (set and rate) applying between two log entries, and thus to enter the drift (rate × time elapsed) experienced since the last entry. If the stream is fast, or changing in direction, each hour's set of the stream since the last water track entry can be recorded. These might then be two (or more) stream lines laid off from the DR arrived at by reference to the water track, to provide the new EP.

Before actually plotting on the chart, all entries in the navigator's log should be *checked*,

(a) from the deck log, for times, log reading, and compass Co.
(b) from the tidal stream atlas (or chart symbols if used).
(c) for arithmetical errors.

If the deck log records any positive fixes obtained—or even good single bearings from which a position line is available, then the EP as at that time should be plotted and compared with the fix or PL. Depending on the navigator's confidence in the bearing(s) recorded, so he will decide whether or not to alter his EP. The observer should be encouraged to note in the deck log his own idea of its accuracy (e.g. 'good', 'rough', 'doubtful', 'Start Pt L/H ???'). If he is satisfied, the navigator will then abandon the EP and mark a fix and plot forward from there.

The column for 'Plot Ref.' is to enable the navigator to 'key' the successive EPs on the chart with the log entries, if he wishes, by letters. Otherwise, the log distance, date and time of each EP and fix should be noted on the chart *astern* of and close to, the EP to which it refers.

Note books

The navigator will be frequently making calculations of various kinds, some simple, some fairly complex, e.g. heights of tide; conversions between compass and true for bearings, courses; distances, speeds, ETAs, fuel stocks and so on. It is recommended that all such calculations are made, and recorded, in a special note book reserved for this purpose. It is surprising how often these will be referred to at a later time for checking, refreshing the memory on how they were done or of noting which ones were wrong, and why.

14. Off to Sea

A successful passage commences with thorough preparation long before departure. Preparations can conveniently be divided into:

(a) Advance preparations which can be made days or weeks in advance.
(b) Departure preparations, requiring attention immediately before leaving.
(c) Preparations en route, those to be worked out during the voyage but before landfall.

Advance preparations

It is a positive pleasure to scan charts and one essential is a chart covering the whole passage (showing departure point and destination) Port approach charts covering any ports likely to be entered through force of circumstances are also needed. Check that all charts are up-to-date, and if not, return them to the chart agent for corrections, shortly before departure.

Pencil in the approximate track from departure to destination, and study the area along this track line, noting the features as described earlier.

Study the sailing directions or pilot covering the area of the passage, and any guide book dealing with the coast and ports en route. Separation zones are set around many headlands and through channels with high shipping density, e.g. Dover Strait, Hook of Holland, Cap Villano (NW Spain),

and others. These prescribe the 'lanes' which certain larger vessels must use while proceeding in either direction. The zones are marked in magenta on Admiralty Charts, and on some (but not all) other charts. They should be treated by the yachtsman as a pedestrian does a motorway. If possible, keep well clear: one can expect a large volume of shipping in them. If proceeding in the same or opposite direction, keep well clear of the lane in shallower water (subject to draft). If crossing a separation zone or shipping lane cross at right angles so as to get across as quickly as possible. Make sure these are shown on the charts to be used, and shape courses accordingly.

Tidal stream atlas

This should be prepared for rapid use in the following manner. Open the atlas at the chartlet for situation at high water. This will be the centre page of the book. Across the top or bottom margin pencil in all the days and dates of the planned passage, and under each, note the times of HW on each day at the port on which the atlas is based. Then work progressively forward and backward through the atlas, changing each pencilled time by one hour (earlier and later) on preceding and succeeding pages. When the stream at any given time and day is required, one has only to flick through the atlas to the chartlet bearing the time nearest to that required on the appropriate day. At the same time, note whether the tides will be springs or neaps over the various days. It is sufficient to indicate this on the centre page only (HW page). This will show whether the springs or the neaps rates of the stream will apply, or enable the rates at times intermediate between springs and neaps to be interpolated.

While preparing the tidal atlas in this way may seem tedious work it is easily done at home. It saves further reference to tide tables and the calculation of the interval between a required time and the time of HW on a given day in order to find the correct chartlet, which otherwise will be necessary at a time when one may be working under stress at sea. It is well worth the initial effort.

Course notes

A study of the rough track line on the chart from departure to destination will suggest the sort of information it will be helpful to have listed up in advance, for quick reference during the passage. (Fig 112.) This will vary widely, depending on the type of passage.

The following lists are recommended for all passages :

(a) List of distances and tentative courses. List the departure point, each headland or landmark to be passed, the mileage between each and the approximate course to steer at each point where an alteration to course will be necessary. The mileage will help in predicting when a landmark should be visible, time along each 'leg', and ETA (Fig 113.). The approximate new course to steer will enable a temporary course to be set immediately, while an accurate course to steer is worked out to allow for the tidal stream at the

LIST OF DISTANCES & TENTATIVE COURSES

Hamble to Dartmouth		A/C to	Mileage	Total	Variation
Needles L/H		245°T	0	0	8°W
Durlstone Hd L/H		,,	14	14	
St Albans Hd 3 m off		,,	4	18	
Portland Bill L/H 6½ m off		263°T	15½	33½	,,
Dartmouth			45	78½	

LIGHTS LIST

		Height	Fog Signals
Needles L/H	Occ: 2 ev 20 sec (sectors)	24m	2 blasts ev 30 sec
Anvil Pt L/H	Fl: ev 10 sec	45m	E.F horn 3 blasts of 2 sec every 30 sec
W. Shambles Lt. By	Fl: 9 ev 15 sec		
Portland Bill L/H	4 Fl: ev 20 sec (sectors)	43m	Diaph 1 bl ev 30 sec
Berry Hd L/H	2 Fl: ev 15 sec	58m	(No fog signals)
Kingswear	Iso W.R.G. sectors (only 318° to 348°)	12 m	
Start Pt L/H	3 Fl: ev 10 sec (& F Red)	62 m	Horn ev 60 sec

PRELIMINARY TIDAL STREAM PLAN

	Miles		Est. Time Hrs 3 kn	6 kn	E.T.A. 3 kn	6 kn	Stream Yacht's Speed 3 kn	6 kn
Needles	0	0	0	0	1930	1930		
Anvil Pt	14	14	4·7	2·3	0010	2145	→1·8	→1·0
St Albans Hd	4	18	6·0	3·0	0130	2230	→1·2	→1·7
Portland Bill	16	34	11·1	5·6	0630	0100	←3·0	→2·0
Dartmouth	45	79	26·0	13·0	2130	0830		

Fig 112. Preparation for a passage. List of distances, courses, the characteristics of marks and tidal streams.

DISTANCES & COURSES
Woodbridge to Plymouth

Miles Cum: Total	Miles to next mark	A/C to M°	
0	0	149°	Deben Entrance
3·4	3·4	145°	Cork L/V Fl. 20 s
			S.W. Bowdsey By. B. 1M to Port
5·4	2·0		Rough By. B.W.H.S. Fl.
			Rough Towers 1·2 M to Stbd.
			Wreck Bys Gp. Fl. 3 & 2 Green ½M to Port
			S. Shipwash By. R.W.H.S Fl. 1M to Port
10·8	5·4	157°	Sunk L/V Gp. Fl (2) 20 s Dia: 2 bl ev min
11·8	1·0		Sunk By. R.W.H.S Fl.
13·0	2·2	128°	Trinity By. B.W. Gp. Fl (4) 15 s. Leave to Port. Whistle.
15·0	2·0	183°	Long Sand Hd. By. B.W. Qk. Fl. Bell w.a.
20·4	5·4		North Knock By. B. (leave 0·8 M. to Stbd)
23·8	3·4	204°	Kentish Knock L/V. Gp. Fl (3) 15 s Dia: 1 bl ev 30 s
			S. Knock By. (unlit) 1 M to Stbd.
			Outer Tongue By. R.W. Qk. Fl. 3 M to Stbd.
			Tongue L/V Gp. Fl (2) 10 s. vis: 9 M. 8 M to Stbd.
41·5	17·7	210°	Elbow By. Gp. Fl (2) 5 s
			N. Foreland L/H. brg: 279 M dist 3·5 M Gp.Fl (5) 20 s
			S. Foreland L/H. brg: 206 M dist 15 M Gp.Fl (3) 20 s
			N. Goodwin L/V brg: 136 M dist 2·5 M Gp.Fl (3) 20 s
			By. RW Gp. Fl (4) Red 1 M to Stbd.
			By. RW Gp. Fl (4) ½M to Port
			By. B Fl. 1 "
			By. RW Qk. Fl ½ "
			By. B Fl. ½ "
			By. B Gp. Fl (3) ½ "
			By. B Fl. ½ "
			By. RW Gp. Fl (2) ¼ "
			By. B Qk Fl ¾ "
51·7	10·2	186°	Buoy Red. Gp. Fl (4)
56·2	4·5	234°	S. Foreland L/H. Gp. Fl (2) 20 s. 2 M due West
76	22		Dungeness L/H. Fl. 10 s. 1 M, N.W.
106	30	267°	Beachy Head L/H. Fl (2) 20 s. 14 M. Expl: ev 5 min
141	35		Owers L/V Fl (3) 20 s. Dia: 3 bl ev min
			Nab Tower Fl. 10 s. Dia: bl ev 2½s & Bell ev 7½ s
165	24	264°	St. Caths L/H. Fl. 5 s. 16 M. Typhon 1 bl ev 45 s
			Needles L/H. Occ (2) 20 s Horn 2 bl ev 30 s
			Anvil Pt. L/H. Fl. 10 s 16 M. EF horn 3 ev 30 s
			Shambles L/F Fl (2) 30 s Horn, N ev 30 s
			Portland Bill Fl (4) 20 s 16 M. Dia: bl ev 30 s

DISTANCES & COURSES (Cont'd)

Miles Cum: Total	Miles to next Mark	A/C to M°	
258	93	265°	Start Pt. L/H. Fl (3) 10 s 19 M Siren bl of 3 s ev min
265	7	309°	(Off Bolt Head)
			E. Rutts By (RYHS) 2·5 M to Port
			Eddystone L/H. Fl (2) 10 s 16 M to Port. Typhon 3 bl ev min
281	16		Plymouth L/H. Fl 10 s 11 M. Bell, 1st every 15 sec
284	3		Cremyll

305·7 kHz		310·3 kHz		291·9 kHz		298·8 kHz	
Falls L/V	FS	Bassurelle L/V	UL	Portland B.	PB	Eddystone	DY*
Tongue L/V	GU	Royal Sov: L/V	RY	St. Caths	CP	Start Pt.	SP
W. Hinder L/V	WH	Pt d'Ailly	AL	C. d'Antifer	TI	Casquets	QS
Ostende	OE	Boulogne	BO	Le Havre	LH	R. Douvres	RD
Calais	CL	C. Griz Nez	GN	Pte de Ver	ER	Ile d Batz	BA
E. Goodwin L/V	GW	Dungeness	DU	Pte Barfleur	FG	Lizard	LZ

312·6 kHz – Cherbourg   * Fog only

Times of High Water

	Woodbridge Haven	Deben Bar	Devonport		Pred: Range	Range
Fri: 21st	0600	0700				
	1835	1935				
Sat: 22nd	0730	0830				
	2000	2100				
Sun: 23rd		0240	14·5 ft	8·3 ft		Sp: 15·4 ft
		1535	14·3			Np: 7·2
Mon: 24th		0350	15·2	9·9		
		1625	15·3			
Tue: 25th		0440	16·0	11·6		
		1710	16·2			

Fig 113. A longer plan for a coastal passage.

actual time, and the leeway according to the actual conditions being experienced.

(b) List of Lights and Fog Signals. (Fig 112 and 113) By reference to the track line on the chart, list all navigational lights expected to be seen at night. Against each, note its characteristics (in full), range, height, note also what sectors are covered, and colour of light if not white. Also note the fog signal of each, its type and characteristics (timing and number of blasts). While doing this, also include details of any light which might be seen if one were off course, or had to enter a port of refuge. Indicate these either by insetting, writing in a different colour, or putting in brackets.

(c) List of DF radio beacons. From a radio beacon chart, or Admiralty List of Radio Signals, Vol. II or from Reed's Nautical Almanac, find and list all radio beacons which will be within radio range of the passage. Bracket together all beacons in the same group (having the same frequency) and note against each its call sign and range.

(d) Port Entry Guide. Any port, harbour or river which may be entered should be closely studied on a large scale chart to plan in advance a safe line or lines of entry. Look up the port in the pilot or other reference book, and note whether any special advice is given.

Port Entry Signals. Some commercial ports are subject to Port Traffic Signal Regulations. The type of signals used, and their exact meaning, should be noted. Where such regulations exist they apply to all vessels, including yachts, and must be complied with. Failure to do so will invoke the wrath of the Harbour Authorities and possibly a fine at least, and at worst will involve the risk of a collision with another vessel, which probably cannot get out of the way. Study the chart and pilot for any approach transits by day, and leading lights by night, including sectors and colours of such lights. Note these carefully, and note also the bearing of such transits or leading lights. One chart is marked :
'Spires of Notre Dame seen in line to right of belfry of Trinity Church 211°'.

A stranger does not know the names of the churches referred to, and may perhaps only be able to pick out a single church. The transit is given as 211°. This is true, so if variation is 9° W, this equals 220° M. Take a compass bearing of the one church seen—say it bears 180° M. Alter course boldly to port, bearing will increase till it is 220° M. Now observe whether a second church is visible roughly in line with the first. If so, the churches can now be identified. If not, real doubt exists as to whether the church seen is either of those referred to, so stand off and seek another. Do not stand on till the situation clarifies.

Where leading lights are placed so that when in transit, in line one over the other, they provide a leading line, it is important to note the bearing of this line. This may be stated in the pilot or on the chart. If not, it can be found by laying off the line through the two lights on the chart. Leading lights are by no means always conspicuous and are sometimes very difficult to identify, particularly in a holiday resort where they can be lost among neon advertisements and hotel lights. A check with the compass bearing should always be applied when any doubt of identification exists.

Buoyage list

Where a study of a large-scale chart of a port indicates it will be necessary to follow a line of buoys, it is recommended that these are listed, preferably by name or number (given on chart, in 'Pilot' or other reference book), the list clearly indicating the shape and colour, and showing the compass bearing from each buoy to the next.

This is particularly useful in wide estuaries where the buoys may be some distance apart. Even when the next buoy can be seen from the last, the compass bearing will immediately confirm whether the one seen is in fact the correct one. If there is any possibility of the port being entered (or left) by night, also list against each buoy its light characteristics, and whether fitted with bell or fog signal.

Preparations on a power boat

Thorough preparations for navigation are just as important for a power yacht as for a sailing craft, possibly even more so in the case of a fast planing power boat. The reason is fairly obvious:

(a) Distances are covered much more quickly, so navigational decisions have to be made correspondingly more quickly.

(b) The motion of the yacht may make reading and writing much more difficult, unless speed is drastically reduced.

(c) Identification of landmarks and buoys is more difficult as each will be in sight for less time, and it may be difficult or impossible to use binoculars. Fixes by hand bearing compass are more difficult and less accurate.

From this it follows that the faster the speed the more detailed the advance preparations should be.

Most coastal and open water passages by fast power boats will be completed within a day, and often within a few hours. The speed can be predicted and thus it should be possible to calculate, in advance, the direction and rate of tidal streams to be dealt with during the passage. Unlike the sailing yacht, in normal sea conditions the power boat can rely on being able to steer any desired course—no tacking is involved. It is therefore possible to prepare accurate courses to

be steered between all turning points.

List of distances and courses

A list should be prepared, similar to that for the sailing yacht but giving actual courses to be steered (instead of only tentative courses). In addition the mileage at each landmark or turning point should be measured and noted, and the total elapsed time from start to each landmark also computed and noted. Except when in a power boat race, the exact time of departure may be uncertain till it actually happens, so total elapsed time to each point may be preferable to recording predicted clock time. If the actual speed is in some doubt, one might have two columns of total elapsed time: one at maximum cruising speed, the other at a reduced speed that might be necessary if sea conditions so dictate. If each column of times is headed with the speed assumed, it is usually easy to interpolate mentally for any intermediate to speed actually sailed. If the yacht's speed is normally controlled by engine revolutions, past experience will enable elapsed times to be calculated and recorded for given r.p.m.s instead of knots.

Engine(s) check list

If there is any possibility of the duration of the passage approaching (or exceeding) the fuel tank capacity, then it might be prudent to calculate what, under normal conditions, the fuel gauge should register at various points on the passage. If the listed turning-points or landmarks are at suitable intervals, the predicted state of fuel stock could be noted against each. Alternatively a separate engine check list should be prepared giving the predicted fuel stock at suitable time intervals, say hourly. The same list can be entered with any routine checks or jobs which should be carried out on a regular schedule, for example, lubricate stern bearing, pump header tank, check water flow, temperature, check ammeters, and so on.

The object of pre-computing fuel stocks is to ensure that warning is available of any undue consumption, to avoid any risk of running out of fuel. Regular and frequent check of all instruments will also give early warning of any possible trouble, on the 'stitch in time' principle.

Buoyage list
A list for each port likely to be entered, similar to that described for slow yachts is even more important for a fast power boat, as there will be little time to consult the chart between buoys.

List of light and fog signals
While not essential for short daylight passages, this list will come into its own if for any reason the passage takes longer than expected, or if fog, mist or heavy rain obstructs visibility. Quick knowledge of the identity of a fog signal from a lighthouse, light vessel or buoy may be vital.

Lists in general
For use on fast power boats, make all lists easy to read under conditions which may be experienced. Bold, clear writing is important.

Check lists
Reverting now to all types of craft, an obvious step to take at the planning stage of a passage is to make check lists. It is annoying, and could be serious, if when well on the way, a chart, reference book or instrument is found to have been forgotten.

Having completed the 'early planning' lists, one is in a position to consider whether the proposed passage or trip fits in with the proposed dates available, and if so, the best time to start.

Factors which are worth consideration are:
(a) What is the rise and fall of the tide at the destination, and the rates of the tidal stream en route? Bear in mind that where the rise and fall is great (e.g. North Brittany) the appearance of the landscape at high water is very different from that at low water, which is the scene depicted by the chart. Tidal streams run strongest at springs, and when flowing against the wind, the stronger the stream the rougher the seas. If this is a first trip, or to an unknown area of large tides, an arrival around neap tides is to be preferred to one at springs, if this can be arranged.
(b) What is the prevailing wind, or most likely direction? If likely to be favourable when outward bound and unfavourable when returning, is there sufficient reserve of time?
(c) Is there an ocean current en route? e.g. Gulf Stream, N Portuguese current. These are shown on routeing charts.

If dates are suitable, the best time of departure can be considered. In some cases this may be immaterial. However, intelligent use of the tidal streams can make all the difference to a passage. The timing should be planned so that the maximum advantage is gained from favourable tidal streams, and that foul streams will be met where they will matter least. For example, if the passage is expected to take about 18 hours, and is along a coast subject to alternate fair and foul tides, the start would probably be planned for just before slack water (high or low as the case might be) before the first favourable tide. One could then expect to have about two favourable and one unfavourable tide. However, the course might lie past a headland where the tide will be strongest, during the period of foul tide. One would weigh up the advisability of timing the passage so that two foul but weak tides would be met, in order to get the benefit of the strongest fair tide past the headland. For this purpose a tidal stream atlas is recommended. Note where the streams run strongest and try to plan times so as to have fair tides at these points or areas.

Departure preparations

Weather—obtain the latest shipping forecast. Phone the local meteorological office, airport or local coast guards, all of whom will normally give you the latest forecast. If available, consult the latest synoptic (weather) chart, to see whether there are any depressions in the offing.

Landfall preparations

Transfer the EP or last fix from the passage chart to the larger scale chart of the destination, as soon as this can be done. This will normally be soon after the landfall has been made. Check the new EP or fix by further observations as soon as any are visible. Work out the height of tide for several hours around the ETA. This may be wanted for clearing shoals when you arrive. The height of tide will certainly be necessary if you propose anchoring, and when that moment arrives you may be too busy to work it out.

It is advisable to calculate the heights at several different hours around the ETA as the last few miles often take longer than expected. You will probably switch on your echo sounder when you approach the 10 fathom line, so remember that depths indicated must be reduced by the height of tide at the time, for comparison with charted depths.

Examine the large-scale chart and work out— well in advance—a safe line of approach, noting what landmarks are likely to be of use, particularly any transits. These may be shown on the chart, or mentioned in any guide or pilot book being used. If entering by night, check for leading lights, note

their compass bearings, and identify as soon as possible. By day, check for leading marks and by day look for any objects on shore which are ahead and in transit. Observation of these will enable the approximate rate and direction of the tidal stream to be estimated. Closer inshore the tidal stream is often running counter to the main stream further out. Check this by also noting how any buoys, lobster pots or vessels at anchor are behaving.

There is a limit to the preparation of courses to be steered, since one cannot predict precisely at what time the yacht will be at any given place— much will depend on the wind and sea encountered. However, the general strategy can be roughed out. Bear in mind :

(a) Landfalls on a well-lit but strange coast are best made just before dawn. The lights can then be positively identified, and the final run into port made in early daylight.

(b) Landfalls on a sparsely lit coast or when visibility is reduced are best made in early daylight to see, and if possible to identify the landmarks. It may be advisable to shape a course so as to close the land a few miles to the left or right of the destination. When land is seen, or a suitable contour line is reached, it is then known which way to turn along the coast to reach the destination.

(c) Identification of a coastline by day can be difficult even when the coast is well-known. If no obvious landmark is visible (such as an identifiable lighthouse or conspicuous building), one hill looks very much like another, and 'wishful thinking' is apt to creep in. Even a headland like the Lizard (S. Cornwall) which once seen one would think never forgotten, looks different seen from different angles. When trying to identify hills, study on the chart their heights, contours and relative distances away. Try to identify three which make as wide an angle between each other as possible. Lay their bearings on the chart, and if the position lines do not cross or make a reasonably small 'cocked hat', they cannot have been correctly identified. When in doubt, stand off and sort things out, never press on if uncertain of the position.

Waypoints

The latitude and longitude of all turning points and check points such as headlands can be listed. They are then fed into the Decca navigator or Loran C set as waypoints and put into sail plan sequence. If the yacht will be sailing in the same waters again, or a return passage passing all or some of the points is contemplated, then the list of lat/longs should be retained. If the set has numerous waypoints, they can even be held in the set and edited into any order. In this case the navigator should have a record of the waypoint numbers against the name of the mark (buoy, beacon, headland or arbitrary position).

Sets will generally compute and supply information on the course and distance between any waypoints, course and distance to next waypoint and distance off track.

15. Coastal Passage

A passage from Hamble to Dartmouth is planned. (Practice chart 5049). No Decca, Loran C nor satellite navigation is on board. The chart shows a course down the West Solent, out past the Needles lighthouse, past Anvil Point, Portland Bill and thence across Lyme Bay to Dartmouth, a total distance of about 96 miles.

The chart shows overfalls of St. Albans Head, and the race off Portland Bill. The tidal stream atlas shows that the stream flows strongly through the Needles channel, and fairly strongly in West Solent. As the Needles channel can be rough, it will be best if this can be traversed at around slack water.

On the proposed day, HW Dover is at 0241 and 1503, the range being about midway between springs and neaps. We want the stream to help us westward down the West Solent, and to be nearly slack, but still helping us, when we reach the Needles. So the stream at the Needles is the determining factor—we should find out at what time the stream will be 'on the turn' (changing from west-going to east-going) at the Needles. Say half an hour before that time will be a good time to reach the Needles. From our tidal stream atlas we see that this occurs about $4\frac{1}{2}$ hours after HW Dover. As HW Dover this day is at 0241 and 1503, this will be at about 0711 and 1933.

Working backwards, the distance from Hamble Point to the Needles is about 16 miles. With a favourable stream averaging about 1 knot we can

fairly assume we shall make at least 5 knots over the ground, so this stretch should take not more than $3\frac{1}{4}$ hrs. We should therefore be at Hamble Point at 0711 minus 315 = say 0400, or 1933 minus 315 = 1615. Allow $\frac{1}{2}$ hour to get from moorings to Hamble Point means we should drop moorings at either 0330 or 1545. Our crew cannot join us till the afternoon, so the latter time is decided on.

As a preliminary plan, we study the chart between the Needles lighthouse and Dartmouth, first checking what danger points (rocks, shoals, races) are near the most direct route. We shall pass close to two rocky headlands (Anvil Point and St Albans Ledge) and not far off Portland Bill. A large-scale chart of these areas, and our pilot book, will warn of a race off St Albans Point, and a tidal race off Portland Bill, both due to strong streams flowing over rocky ledges. It will therefore be prudent to give both a good berth, and particularly Portland Bill.

We can now make a tentative tidal stream plan (Fig 112.) for the passage from the Needles to Dartmouth. (We can omit the short 16 mile trip down the Solent.) As we want to keep well off Portland Bill we draw an arc of a circle, radius, say, 6 miles and centre Portland Bill lighthouse, and a track line from Needles lighthouse to the southern edge of the arc. We note that this line passes some $2\frac{1}{2}$ miles south of Anvil Point and well clear of St Albans Ledge. From the point on

175

the arc we draw the track to Dartmouth entrance. We can now scale off the distances with dividers. The next step is to arrive at a fair assessment of the streams we can expect, particularly at those places where the tidal stream is likely to be fastest. We do not know what speed we shall make under sail, so we could make the list for two speeds:

(a) If there are head winds, or light winds.
(b) If there is a good 'free' wind.

We might assume that we shall make either 3 knots, or 6 knots. Working from our expected departure time from the Needles of 1930 Friday, we can calculate the times (at both 3 kn and 6 kn) required to cover each 'leg' and thus the times we are likely to reach each salient point.

Referring now to our tidal stream atlas, on which we should have pencilled in the times each chartlet will apply, we can note on our preliminary plan the directions, and approximate rates, of the streams. We see that there is a foul (east-going) stream at Anvil Point and St Albans Head. If we make poor progress the stream will have turned fair (west-going) off Portland Bill, but will still be foul there if we make good time. We cannot predict our ETA at Dartmouth with any certainty, but the Lyme Bay crossing of some 45 miles is bound to take anything from seven to fifteen hours, so we shall experience more than one tide. Fortunately the stream across a large bay is usually fairly slack so we can, at this stage, disregard it. Note however that when we are within striking distance of Dartmouth (say 15–20 miles off) we must then decide what the tidal stream will be doing for the remainder of the passage, to ensure we do not get set off course.

Reviewing our tidal stream plan, it seems that the initial track is suitable. By passing 2–3 miles

DECK LOG

Date BST	Log Rdg	Course Reqd.	Co steered since last entry	Wind	Baro	Remarks
Fri/1605				W2	1002	Dropped moorings Hamble under engine
1630				WNW3		Hamble Pt Buoy. Engine off. Made sail, No.1 Genoa
1810					1000	Hamsted Ledge Buoy
1925	0	256°	256°	W4		Needles L/H ½ m to S.E. Streamed log.
2000	2·6	"	256°	W4	998	
2150	12·2	"				Needles L/H just dipping Anvil Pt L/H brg 310°M = 302°T
2200	12·9	"	256°	WSW5	996	4 rolls in Main, set no.2 Genoa headed steering 250° stbd. tack
2400	21·7	"	250°	"	1000	
Sat/0200	30·6	"	248°	"	1004	Rain
0400	39·3	"	252°	W4	1008	Portland Bill L/H obs: 340°M (good) wind veering, set whole Main
0600	48·3	263°	255°	WNW4	1008	Tacked to Port tack
0800	57·7	"	341°	NW4	1010	Tacked to Starboard tack laying about 260°
1000	67·7	"	265°	NNW3	1014	Freed sheets, set no.1 Genoa
1200	78·5	273°	273°	"	"	
1245	82·8	"	273°			High ground seen, bearing appro 310°M
1330	87·1	"				H.S.A's taken. Start Pt. L/H 6=° Beacon 39°, Berry Hd.
1450	94·2	"				Picked up mooring Dartmouth

Fig 114. Deck log, as it appears.

off the first two headlands we shall escape the strongest area of the then foul tide. If we make a fast passage we shall hit a foul tide off Portland Bill, but going further south will not greatly reduce the tidal stream and only add mileage. On the other hand, if we make a slow passage it may pay us to stand in a little closer to get more advantage from the then favourable (west-going) stream. This we can only decide when we are passing St Albans Head, or thereabouts.

The passage

We are all aboard, all gear checked against lists and stowed, and ready to sail. We motor off, entering the deck log (Fig 114.). The passage down the west Solent calls for no navigation, the courses steered being determined by eye, by reference to the buoys which are identified on the large-scale chart. This is pilotage.

At the Needles the patent log is set to zero and streamed. On the way we have noted that the wind is about west, so we should be able to lay our course past Anvil Point sailing full and bye. We set 256° C (which will give a water track of 245° T (see navigator's log, Fig 115.). Entries in the Navigator's Log can now start.

We propose working up the EP every 2 hours, but at 2150 the helmsman reports (and logs) that he has seen Needles light (astern) just dip, and has also taken a hand bearing compass bearing of Anvil Point light bearing 310° M. The Lights list shows Needles being 24 m high, our height of eye is 1·5 m, so the distance off is 13 miles (from Table of Rising and Dipping Distances). This gives the navigator his first fix, so it will not be necessary to plot the run so far: merely to mark the fix on the chart, with time and date.

At 2200 the wind has piped up and sail is reduced (and this is logged). At 2400 the deck log shows

NAVIGATOR'S LOG

Date	Time BST	Log Rdg	Log Since last plot	C°	Course Dev E+ W-	Var E+ W-	T°	Lee Way P+ S-	Water Track True	Tidal Stream Set °	Rate kn	Drift m	Plot Ref	Lat / Long
Fri	1925	0												
	2150	12·2	12·2	256	2 E	8 W	250	S -5	245°	225	0·5	0·7		O.P. 50°33·3 N, 1°53·8 W
	2400	21·7	9·5	250	2 E	8 W	244	S -5	239°	090	2·0	4·0		
Sat	0200	30·6	8·9	248	2 E	8 W	242	S -5	237°	080	1·5	3·0		
	0400	39·3	8·7	252	2 E	8 W	246	S -5	241°	095	0·5	1·0		Portland Bill LH obs 340 M=332 T
	0600	48·3	9·0	255	2 E	8 W	249	S -5	244°	240	1·6	3·2		
	0800	57·7	9·4	341	2 W	8 W	335	P +5	340°	260	1·5	3·0		
	1000	67·7	10·0	265	2 E	8 W	259	S -5	254°	040	0·3	0·6		
	1200	78·5	10·8	273	2 E	9 W	266	S -5	261°	030	0·6	1·2		
	1330	87·1	8·6										HSA	O.P. 50°17·7 N, 3°25·2 W

Fig 115.   Navigator's log entered up.

TIDAL STREAM PLAN

Alderney to Poole Harbour, (2 miles east of Anvil Point)

Yacht Speed 8 kn. Distance 53 m.
H.W. Dover 2130 & 0950 B.S.T.

B.S.T.	From H.W. Dover	1st Approximation		2nd Approximation	
2230	1 hour after	240°	3 knots	240°	3 knots
2330	2 ,, ,,	240°	4 ,,	240°	4 ,,
0030	3 ,, ,,	240°	3 ,,	250°	4 ,,
0130	4 ,, ,,	240°	2·5 ,,	250°	3 ,,
0230	5 ,, ,,	260°	1·0 ,,	260°	1 ,,
0330	6 ,, ,,	070°	0·4 ,,	080°	0·5 ,,
0400	6 hours before	050°	1·0 ,,	095°	0·6 ,,
0500	5 ,, ,,			090°	2·8 ,,
0600	4 ,, ,,			040°	2·7 ,,

Fig 116.   Tidal stream notes for a power boat. Since it can be gauged, where she will be each hour.

that the wind has backed slightly and the helmsman has recorded that the best course he has been able to maintain since 2200 has averaged 250° C. Navigator's log is entered from the deck log, and the stream experienced since 2150 is assessed from the tidal stream atlas and entered. To save work, the results from the two nearest tidal pages is used, rather than each single hour's tidal stream separately. The error is unlikely to be significant. The run (water track) and tidal drift are plotted and the 2400 hrs EP marked on the chart.

At 0200 the log is read and the helmsman enters the average course he has steered since the last entry—248° C. The navigator's log is entered and the new EP worked up and charted as before.

At 0400 the deck log shows the helmsman was able to get a bearing of Portland Bill lighthouse. The EP is worked up as before, and the position line from the lighthouse is also plotted. Assuming this is a reliable observation it is evident that the position must be somewhat ahead of the EP. Possibly the adverse stream was slightly over-estimated. The 0400 position can therefore be moved forward, parallel with the track line, to the position line just established from the bearing of the lighthouse.

Shortly after 0400 the wind veers and the helmsman is ordered to continue sailing close-hauled, to head up as high into the wind as possible consistent with making good way. At 0600 he records his average has been 255° C. This is worked up and plotted. It now seems that the passage will take another 8 hours or so. The stream will be going NE for the next couple of hours, then SW for about 6 hours. It seems prudent to go on to port tack to work up to nearer the original track line.

The 0800 EP puts the yacht's position almost on the original rhumbline. A further veer in

the wind can be expected, deduced from the barometer readings, which suggests the passing of a depression, so the yacht is put on starboard tack.

The 1000 EP shows the destination is about due west, and the wind has veered further, allowing the course for Dartmouth to be steered, sailing free. The distance is about 21 miles, or 4 hours sailing, during which the stream will be flowing about 020° at $\frac{1}{2}$ kn average. A two-hour tidal vector is drawn, giving a water track required of 261° T on starboard tack. The navigator enters this in his log, under water track, and working 'backwards' to the left, arrives at a course to steer, 273° C, which he gives the helmsman and notes in the deck log under 'course required'.

At 1245 high ground is seen fine on the starboard bow, and at 1330 the beacon east of Dartmouth, Start Point lighthouse and Berry Head lighthouse can all be identified. Horizontal sextant angles of these three are taken: Start Point lighthouse 065° Kingswear Beacon 039° Berry Head lighthouse.

Plotting these puts the yacht's position some two miles south of the EP, at 50° 17·7′N, 3° 25·2′W. This is confirmed by an echo sounder reading which, when the height of tide is subtracted from it, gives a sounding of 51 m.

The large-scale chart of Dartmouth is now brought out and the fix just obtained transferred to it by Lat. and Long. This is studied to establish a safe line of approach and to note any channel buoys or leading marks. From here on the navigator's task is again pilotage, picking up and identifying landmarks (the Mewstone, 35 m high) and conning the yacht into a safe mooring or anchorage. Leading marks shown on the chart will be identified as early as possible, and care taken to ensure that any cross-tidal stream is allowed for to keep the yacht on the leading line. If no

Position by dead reckoning

 Estimated position

 A fix by landmarks, radio or celestial sights

 Water track

 Ground track

 Tidal stream or current

 A position line

A transferred position line

 A range circle

NAVIGATOR'S SYMBOLS
These symbols are found convenient by navigators for working on their charts. They are drawn and at the conclusion of the passage are rubbed out. They are not to be found printed anywhere. There is nothing to prevent you inventing your own system, but obviously if just lines and crosses are used for all workings, it will be difficult to understand them an hour or two later.

leading marks are visible, a transit of two objects ahead will be used to guard against sideways drift off the safe approach line.

The height of tide will be pre-calculated for 1400 and 1500 so that echo sounder depths can be rapidly reduced to soundings for comparison with chart depths. The most suitable anchorage will be earmarked in advance, or it may be decided to moor at the marina. If the yacht is anchored, the proper anchor scope for the depth and tidal range will be checked, and as soon as the anchor is down, cross bearings will be taken so that, if it comes on to blow, any tendency to drag can be seen.

A coastal passage for a displacement power boat

Let us assume our yacht has a comfortable cruising speed of 8 knots, and we are planning a passage from Alderney (Braye Harbour) to Poole. Not being dependent on the wind we can (provided it is not unduly strong) lay any course we decide on. We should make similar preparations before departure to those described in the previous pages, including a list of lights likely to be seen or required, and we should work out a tidal stream plan for the predicted tides during the period of the proposed crossing.

Assume we decide to make a night crossing, arriving about dawn so as to have the benefit of lighthouses for our landfall. First we pencil in on the chart the rhumbline or track course required, from Braye Harbour to a point 2 mile east of Anvil Point. If we can make that position we shall be (in reasonable visibility) within sight of Poole Bar Buoy. The track Co is 012° T, distance 53 miles. Disregarding tidal streams, this would take just under 7 hours. (Fig 116.)

Knowing the streams run strongly, we must allow for them in deciding on the water track

required. If we wished, we could lay off a series of courses to allow for the constantly changing streams, so as to maintain the yacht on the rhumbline. If the course would take us near dangers this might be necessary, and would involve drawing a tidal vector for each successive hourly stream direction and rate, with a series of different courses to be steered. The passage under discussion is in open water, and once clear of Alderney there are no dangers till we make our landfall. There is therefore no advantage in making frequent alterations to the course to keep on the rhumbline, and we can calculate a single course which (if the streams run as predicted and we maintain a set speed through the water) should bring us to our destination. Using the dividers opened to 8 miles (yacht's proposed speed) mark along the rhumbline 8-mile marks.

Departure is planned for 2130 HW Dover this day is 2100, just before springs. Write down the times from 2200 to 0400, and against each write the 'Hrs after (or before) HW'. Now opening the tidal atlas at the first 'Hrs from HW' (in our case 1 hr after HW Dover) note down what the stream will be doing in the first hour's stretch of the rhumbline. Turning to the next hour page in the tidal atlas and judging by eye where the second hour's stretch on the rhumbline will lie on the tidal chartlet, note this new stream. Repeat till 0400 and the last stretch of the rhumbline has been dealt with.

From the departure point (entrance to Braye Harbour, Alderney) lay off each of the tidal stream lines listed, progressively, from the end of the last one plotted. (As the tidal stream in each of the first four hours is predicted to be setting in the same direction (240° T), a single tidal stream line 12·5 miles long will suffice, for this stretch).

With centre the end of the composite tidal stream line, and radius the distance through the water the yacht will travel in seven hours ($8 \times 7 = 56M$) describe an arc to cut the rhumbline. This will give the direction of the water track. (If the dividers will not span 56 miles, halve the length of the composite tidal stream line, and halve the distance through the water. The water track direction will be the same but half the length). The water track will be found to be 022° T and the distance made good in 7 hrs will be 48 miles, speed made good over the ground 6·85 knots. We can now see that it will take us appreciably longer than seven hours to reach our destination, because the tidal stream, on average, will be partly against us.

We can now do a more accurate tidal plan, based on making good about 6·8 knots (in place of the original 8). Rub out the first tidal vector and hourly stretches along the rhumbline and replace this with hourly stretches each 6·8 miles long, and list the expected streams in these revised areas each hour (see under second approximation). We now find we have a composite streams line covering 9 hours, and a new water track of 018½° T, distance made good 60 miles in 9 hrs = 6·7 knots.

Finally, we convert the water track to course to steer by applying leeway (if any), variation and deviation in the usual way. Leeway we can only assess when we are at sea and can gauge what leeway the wind is likely to produce.

Note that the rhumbline was   012° T
Water track by first approx.   022° T
Water track by second approx.   018½° T

If no allowance had been made for the streams the yacht would have reached the coast about 9 miles west of the desired position (well into Weymouth Bay). If the course had been set for the first approximation she would have made landfall about 3 miles to the west, and Anvil Point lighthouse would have appeared on her starboard bow instead of to port.

The course to steer is now known, but it is still necessary to keep a proper deck log and to plot the EP at regular intervals. It may well be necessary to alter course, or the speed may be varied, for any number of reasons. If a large fishing fleet is encountered it may be necessary to make a wide detour round it; rough seas or reduced visibility may require speed to be reduced, engine trouble may occur, and so on. While it may not be necessary to make frequent plots on the chart, it is still important to have all the data recorded (time, course, distance run by log, etc.) so that an EP can be plotted whenever necessary.

Before landfall, calculate the approximate height of tide so as to be able to reduce soundings to chart datum for comparing echo sounder with chart depths. Calculate when Anvil Point lighthouse should be visible. If it does not appear when predicted, watch the echo sounder. After landfall has been made, lose no opportunity of checking how the stream is setting, by any transits visible, lobster pot buoys, etc. Allow for this when piloting into harbour and guard against being set across the course by taking bearings ahead with the hand bearing compass. Watch the echo sounder. Have heights of tide pre-calculated for Poole Harbour. These will be useful both for reductions to soundings and for deciding where to anchor, if this planned. As harbour is approached, change to a large-scale chart, and note the buoyage system.

16. Blinded but not Lost: Fog!

Boating in fog is an eerie and unnerving experience. All sense of direction is lost and even the sea level appears to change as there is no horizon to establish a level. At night the glow of the navigation lights reflected in the fog seems to close one in, and one can even get the sensation that the yacht is sailing downhill.

The official definition of fog is an atmospheric condition which reduces visibility to 1000 metres or less. It is said to be 'mist' when visibility is between 1000 and 2000 metres. There are a number of types of fog due to different causes, but the end effect is moisture in saturated air condensing out into minute droplets which reduce the transmission of light. Once out of sight of land it is very difficult to gauge the visibility distance. One must be alert to the possibility of something suddenly emerging out of mist or fog at much shorter range than expected. If a buoy is passed, it is a good idea to get an estimate of the visibility by taking the time or reading the log when it is close abeam and again when it disappears, and (allowing for tidal stream) thus to calculate the distance.

It is better to avoid fog than to have to deal with it. Pilot books, routeing charts and other sea guides give indications of the prevalence or likelihood of fog at different times of year. Radio weather and shipping forecasts give reliable warnings of the likelihood of fog, weather reports from coastal stations state if fog is present, and give the visibility, usually in yards. If in port, a passage may be postponed if fog is present or forecast for any part of the voyage. There is always an element of danger when at sea in fog or mist. As with most aspects of sailing, thorough preparation, in advance, will go far to reduce the inevitable anxiety. The very knowledge of navigation will mean that the yacht is steered confidently: sudden feelings that 'we must be near land' or 'I am sure we are heading in the wrong direction' disappear as this confidence grows.

The two hazards in fog are the risks of collison and of running aground. Preparations for dealing with fog should not be deferred till visibility has deteriorated to the official fog visibility of 1,100 metres or less, but should be put in hand the moment visibility shows signs of deteriorating. This is not always easy to detect if one is not sailing within sight of land, buoys or other vessels, so an eye should be kept on the sharpness of the horizon. Preparation will be more sure if a check list has been prepared in advance. This might read as follows:

1. Obtain fix by visual observation if possible, or electronic means.
2. Switch on echo sounder, read and record depth and time.

3. Post lookout(s).
4. Hoist radar reflector.
5. Issue life jackets to all hands.
6. Prepare flares.
7. Sound fog signals per rules.
8. Prepare anchor for immediate letting go.
9. Prepare liferaft or dinghy.
10. Check engine.
11. Warn helmsman to maintain accurate course as ordered.
12. Navigator to lay off safest course, and order.
Let us go through these points in detail.
1. Obtain fix. If using Decca etc. there is no difference due to fog, though the position will be plotted more frequently. Without Decca the last visual position before fog closed in is very important, as dead reckoning will have to be relied on until it clears. If no reliable fix by visual observation is possible, when visibility closes in, then the EP should be worked up, as accurately as possible, from the last fix or EP. If well within the range of any radio DF station(s), the EP should be confirmed with bearings so obtained. Bear in mind that some DF stations which do not operate in clear weather will now be working in fog.
2. Switch on echo sounder. This should be left running throughout fog (if within soundings). The navigator should calculate the height of tide (to a half a metre) and should reduce the depth to CD and should check this with his fix or EP. Depth readings should be taken and recorded (with times and patent log readings) at regular and frequent intervals. The intervals will be governed by the type of coastline (shelving or steep-to) and on the yacht's speed.
3. Lookouts. One man should be posted right in the bows, to have a clear view and to be as far from engine noise as possible. He should be instructed to report everything seen or heard, and to indicate direction by *pointing* with the whole arm. This is the quickest and surest way of indicating to the helmsman or skipper. If the size of the crew permits, others should be detailed to watch each beam and astern. Order absolute silence.
4. Radar reflector. It is almost more important to be seen than to see, so ensure the radar reflector is correctly hoisted and well up. If caught out without a radar reflector aboard, hoist a metal bucket or wet the sails by throwing water on them as high as possible. This will at least help to produce some trace on another vessel's radar display.
5. Lifejackets. These should be worn (and if of the inflatable type, blown up) by all hands. If by any chance you were involved in a collision, these might make all the difference between being picked up, and not.
6. Flares. If sailing at night, these should be used (white flares) if a vessel's lights are seen on a possible collision course.
7. Fog Signals. Rule 33(a) of the international collision regulations specifies these: 'A power driven or sailing vessel of 12 m or over, to carry a fog horn sounded by mechanical means, and a bell'; and 'A power driven or sailing vessel of less than 12 m to be capable of making "some other efficient sound signal".' Rule 35 lays down the sound signals required in fog. These must be known by heart so that not only can you make the correct signal, but that you know, by her signals, what another vessel is doing. For the larger yacht over 12 m, sounding signals should present no problem. The smaller yacht under 12 m should carry either:
(a) An aerosol-powered pressure horn,
(b) A hand-pump powered horn, or
(c) A mouth-blown horn.
The range of any of these is limited, and will depend on atmospheric conditions, but is

Fog soon turns simple pilotage into a baffling problem. A
single marked post provides a clue to channel in an estuary.

Same scene, but with the fog having lifted. Landmarks and
further navigational markers can now be seen.

practical yacht navigator

Normal view towards shore of an estuary with visibility several miles.

Fog clamps down visibility to about two hundred metres. Shore line is just discernible, but not trees behind it and it is even more difficult than usual to judge distance.

unlikely to exceed (a) and (b) a mile, and (c) a few hundred yards at best. The aerosol-horn is probably the most practical for the smaller yacht as it is small, light and easily stowed and used. However, one aerosol container will not produce more than 250 to 300 blasts, so it is advisable to time the frequency of the blasts with these limitations in mind. If under sail (no engine) one long followed by two short blasts every minute are required by rule 35(c). At this rate, one aerosol container would last little more than one hour, and the yacht may be in fog for much longer than this. In waters crowded with traffic, entering a port or estuary frequented by shipping, the signals should be given at the regulation one-minute intervals, but in open waters the intervals should be more spaced out to ensure capacity for sounding on hearing the fog signal of another vessel.

If anchored, remember to sound at one minute intervals the bell, or if not carried, strike a frying pan, bucket or the suspended kedge anchor (which 'rings' well).

8. Anchor. An anchor or kedge should be ready on deck with some cable or warp veered (flaked out on deck), so that the yacht can be anchored quickly if necessary.

9. Prepare dinghy. As the possibility exists of being run down by a large vessel in fog, it is prudent to make preparations 'just in case'. If a self-inflating raft is carried, this should be freed from its holding-down lashings, but NOT inflated. But check that the rip-cord/painter is securely attached to the yacht. It is probably wise to launch a rigid dinghy carried on deck—it can be put back when the fog has cleared. A packed inflatable dinghy which is not self-inflating should certainly be fully inflated and either carried right-way-up on deck, or towed aft. Paddles, flares and food and water should be placed aboard and secured, or put in a handy bag ready.

10. Engine. In a power-driven yacht, the engine should be given a quick check, particularly fuel supply, as it is essential to have full power available if it should be necessary to take rapid avoiding action. As the navigator must know his position continuously, it is important that a steady speed can be maintained. In a yacht under sail, if the wind is sufficient to maintain at least three knots, it may be preferable to continue sailing as the absence of engine noise will enable another ship's, and navigational, fog signals to be heard at much greater distances. If the wind is very light—as it often (but not always) is in fog—the engine should be started and a steady speed maintained.

Rule 19 of International Regulations for Preventing Collisions at sea deals with conduct of vessels in restricted visibility. Subsection (b) requires every vessel to proceed at a safe speed adapted to the prevailing circumstances. 'A power driven vessel shall have her engines ready for immediate manoeuvre'. 19(d) lays down what to do in the event of sighting by radar alone. Under 19(e) 'every vessel which hears apparently forward of her beam the fog signal of another vessel, shall reduce her speed to the minimum'.

Let us consider the 'circumstances'. A yacht's auxiliary is apt to be temperamental and may be difficult to re-start when hot. A large vessel stops by going full astern, but her stopping distance may be a mile or more. She has a very wide turning circle. If a yacht meets a large vessel at close quarters, the yacht's best chance of avoiding a collision will usually be by alteration of course. She has a very small turning circle (often not much more than her own length) and she will 'stop' her forward progress most quickly by going about under full helm and full power.

If another vessel's fog horn is first heard

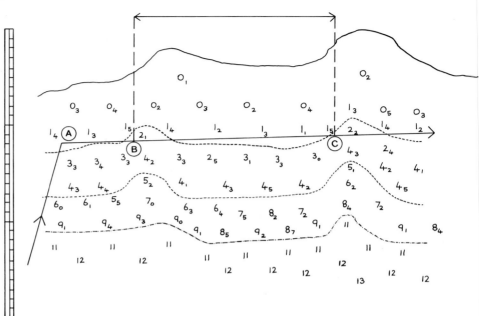

Fig 117. Planning a course in fog. It is intended to stay in the shallow water: distance run between B and C is checked by log.

apparently fairly distant, it may be prudent to slow the engine down to reduce engine-noise and thus to give the forward look-out the best chance of gauging the direction of the other vessel.
Remember that the other vessel should sound-off every two minutes. Unless the fog is extremely dense, it is advisable not to alter course on first hearing another vessel's fog horn, but to hold course and speed, with redoubled vigilance. If she comes into sight heading straight for your yacht, turn AWAY from her at full throttle and head at about 90° from her approximate track. If she ought to pass ahead, ALSO turn away so as to escape her wash. Only hold your course if you are SURE she will pass astern of you. NEVER attempt to cross her bows.

11. Warn helmsman to maintain course ordered. All sense of direction is lost in fog. As the navigator must rely on the course steered and distance covered to keep track of the yacht's position, accurate steering is most important. The navigator must keep in mind his own ship's heading and the most probable heading of vessels met so as to be able to make a quick decision if necessary. If a quick alteration to course is made, new course, time and log reading should be logged at the earliest opportunity and no reliance placed on memory.

12. Navigator's duties. After getting his fix or EP on the chart and entering it in the log (with time and patent log reading), his next task is to lay off the safest possible course. This will depend on circumstances.

(a) *If in enclosed waters,* in a buoyed shipping channel or a harbour approach, immediately get out of the fairway by steering for the nearest bank. Watch the echo sounder. If the fog is dense, the safest course will be to anchor in shoal water. If visibility is not less than about a quarter the distance between channel buoys it may be reasonable to lay a course from one buoy to the next, bearing in mind any cross-current, and taking care to keep on the out-of-channel side of the line. If a buoy is missed and there is shipping about it is prudent to turn into shallow water and anchor rather than to 'guess' where the next buoy may be.

(b) *If coasting.* If along a shelving shore (contour lines far apart) and without offlying rocks, lay a course direct to shoal water (allowing for the approximate height of tide when reading the echo sounder) so as to be out of the reach of most vessels. Then proceed along a contour line by compass and echo sounder. Better still, lay off a course on the chart which is a straight line for a reasonable distance and one which conforms to the safe soundings decided on. In Fig 117 it should be possible to detect fairly accurately when the yacht reaches point A, then point B and point C, by noting when the depths increase to those charted, and checking that the distances on the chart correspond to the distance run by log (corrected for tidal stream). If the fog is very dense or there are rocks about, it is clearly more prudent to anchor till visibility lifts.

If along a steep-to shore (deep soundings on the chart close to the shore) or with offlying rocks, set a course parallel to, or slightly away from land and warn lookouts to listen for breakers. Watch the echo sounder much more frequently.

(c) *If well off-shore.* Try to estimate the position of shipping lanes. Then lay a course to cross such lanes at a right angle so as to get across and away from them as quickly as possible.

Throughout, the navigator must ensure the deck log is maintained meticulously—course steered, time and log reading of every alteration to course, and of fog signals heard to help him gauge shipping lanes. He should plot his EP carefully at suitable intervals—the nearer land the more frequently. He should pay particular attention to tidal streams, bearing in mind that whether the yacht is moving or stopped in the water (but not when anchored) the tidal stream will have the same effect. In fog the wind is often light and the sea calm. Streams are likely to conform closely to predictions. If carefully worked up, the positions found by dead reckoning (plus streams) are likely to be most reliable. However, nothing should be left to chance, and EPs should be checked by radio DF and soundings, but when these are not available, trust your EP.

If in coastal waters the navigator should make a list (if he has not already done so in the course of his normal pre-passage work) of lighthouses, light vessels and buoys, listing their fog signal characteristics and type. All radio DF stations and aero beacons likely to come within range should be listed, with times and identification letters. If distant more than about half their listed range, treat a position so found with caution, particularly at night or twilight when distortion or refraction is at a maximum. Warn all hands that the direction and the distance off of all sound signals in fog can be extremely misleading. Bear this in mind when deciding on action on hearing a fog signal.

Maxims to remember in fog or mist are:

1. Constant lookout: including astern and abeam.
2. Maintain silence: no unavoidable talking.
3. Watch echo sounder (in soundings).
4. Hold a steady compass course and speed.
5. Turn away from danger.
6. Plot the EP frequently, and trust the EP till proved wrong.
7. Sound fog signals in accordance with international collision regulations, rule 35.

The use of Decca or Loran C obviously makes the whole fog navigational situation quite different. With the position known exactly, many other problems do not ensue; for instance it may be known that big ships will not be on course for the yacht. Many of the other precautions mentioned above still apply and all of them on a vessel without electronic aids.

17. Traverse Tables

When we are using a chart to plot successive EPs we do so by laying off a line representing direction and distance sailed through the water, add a tidal stream line if appropriate, and the end of the line gives a new EP. We can read its latitude and longitude from the edges of the chart. If we are making frequent alterations to course steered, as when tacking to windward or sailing on wind shifts, we have to plot a series of runs in different directions and distances. We may be subject to a series of tidal streams setting in varying directions and rates. We can again, if we wish, lay off each individual 'run' on a given course, and lay off each tidal stream line of appropriate length and direction. We can find the latitude and longitude of the final position reached, or if we wish, any intermediate position. This can be a tedious process, and each separate line provides its individual element of small error.

If we are in the middle of an ocean, or making a long semi-coastal passage we shall probably be using a small-scale chart covering several hundred miles. A run of a score or so of miles, or a tidal stream line for a few hours would be too small to plot accurately and we shall need to calculate (rather than to plot on the chart) the change in position and thus the new position, in terms of its latitude and longitude.

The Traverse Tables are a quick means of enabling us to calculate a new EP after a single run, or a series of separate runs and/or tidal streams, from our original EP, or a fix or observed position, without the necessity for plotting, or indeed without the use of a chart at all.

The tables

In navigation, positions are described in terms of their latitude and longitude. This could be said to be a form of map grid reference: so many degrees and minutes N or S of the equator: so many W or E of the Greenwich meridian 0°. The point described is at the intersection of the two. Except when the course happens to be exactly N or S, E or W, we are always 'traversing' across the chart, diagonally.

If we sail from A to C, (Fig 118.), a distance of, say, 10 miles, we shall have made some northing and some easting. The amount of northing will be A–B, and the easting B–C. We have a right-angled triangle. We know the angle 'a', the course, and the side A–C, the distance. The traverse tables will tell us the length of the other two sides A–B and B–C. If one sails a course of 320° (N40°W) from a known position, say 30°N 25°W, what will be the position after sailing 50 miles? Clearly one has sailed a certain amount northward, so the N latitude will have increased, and a certain amount westward, so the longitude will have increased. But by how much? This is the sort of problem the traverse table solves.

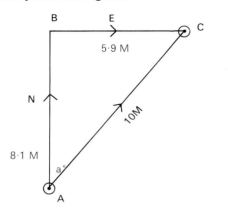

Fig 118. Yacht goes 10 miles from A to C: traverse tables will find change in latitude and longitude. For course a°, 36° and distance 10M, A–B is 'D.Lat.' 8·1M, B–C is 'departure' 5·9 M.

In Fig 118, assume the yacht is at position A, latitude 54°N, longitude 3°E and sails 10 miles on course 036° (N36°E). What is the latitude and longitude of the final position C? The traverse tables solve the right-angled triangle ABC.

But first we must consider the units used. We know that, by definition, one 1' of *latitude* = 1 nautical mile. But we also know that 1' of *longitude* does NOT equal a nautical mile—only on the equator. It is obvious from a globe that as we move further away from the equator the distance in miles between two meridians of longitude becomes less and less, till they meet at the poles. So the number of minutes of longitude spanned by a mile depends on the *latitude* of the position. The Traverse Tables give the answer to our right-angled triangle in terms of miles both ways. In the diagram, C is so many miles (= minutes of latitude) north of A (A to B), and so many miles (but *not* minutes of longitude) east of A (B to C). The *miles* moved in a easterly or westerly direction are called *departure*.

The traverse tables have 45 double pages, each headed with degrees from 1° up to 45°. Fig 119 gives a single page for 36° as an example. This is a left-hand page and covers Distances from 1 to 300 miles. The right-hand page (not illustrated) covers Distances from 301 to 600 miles. Note that each block of columns is headed '*D.Lon–Dep*', and underneath '*Dist.–D.Lat–Dep*'. For the moment, disregard '*D.Lon. Dep*'. The course in our example was 36°, and distance 10 miles. On Traverse Table page for 36° against Dist. 10 we find D. lat. 8·1 and Dep. 5·9. This means that, on this course, the difference in latitude (D. lat.) between A and B will be 8·1 miles (= 8'·1 of lat.) and the change in an easterly direction will be 5·9 MILES of departure.

Table 3	TRAVERSE TABLE		36°

36°

D Lon	Dep		D Lon	Dep		D Lon	Dep		D Lon	Dep		D Lon	Dep	
Dist.	D. Lat.	Dep.	Dist.	D. Lat.	Dep.	Dist.	D. Lat.	Dep.	Dist.	D. Lat.	Dep.	Dist.	D. Lat.	Dep.
Hyp.	Adj.	Opp.	Hyp.	Adj.	Opp.	Hyp.	Adj.	Opp.	Hyp.	Adj.	Opp.	Hyp.	Adj.	Opp.
1	0.8	0.6	61	49.4	35.9	121	97.9	71.1	181	146.4	106.4	241	195.0	141.7
2	1.6	1.2	62	50.2	36.4	122	98.7	71.7	182	147.2	107.0	242	195.8	142.2
3	2.4	1.8	63	51.0	37.0	123	99.5	72.3	183	148.1	107.6	243	196.6	142.8
4	3.2	2.4	64	51.8	37.6	124	100.3	72.9	184	148.9	108.2	244	197.4	143.4
5	4.0	2.9	65	52.6	38.2	125	101.1	73.5	185	149.7	108.7	245	198.2	144.0
6	4.9	3.5	66	53.4	38.8	126	101.9	74.1	186	150.5	109.3	246	199.0	144.6
7	5.7	4.1	67	54.2	39.4	127	102.7	74.6	187	151.3	109.9	247	199.8	145.2
8	6.5	4.7	68	55.0	40.0	128	103.6	75.2	188	152.1	110.5	248	200.6	145.8
9	7.3	5.3	69	55.8	40.6	129	104.4	75.8	189	152.9	111.1	249	201.4	146.4
10	8.1	5.9	70	56.6	41.1	130	105.2	76.4	190	153.7	111.7	250	202.3	146.9
11	8.9	6.5	71	57.4	41.7	131	106.0	77.0	191	154.5	112.3	251	203.1	147.5
12	9.7	7.1	72	58.2	42.3	132	106.8	77.6	192	155.3	112.9	252	203.9	148.1
13	10.5	7.6	73	59.1	42.9	133	107.6	78.2	193	156.1	113.4	253	204.7	148.7
14	11.3	8.2	74	59.9	43.5	134	108.4	78.8	194	156.9	114.0	254	205.5	149.3
15	12.1	8.8	75	60.7	44.1	135	109.2	79.4	195	157.8	114.6	255	206.3	149.9
16	12.9	9.4	76	61.5	44.7	136	110.0	79.9	196	158.6	115.2	256	207.1	150.5
17	13.8	10.0	77	62.3	45.3	137	110.8	80.5	197	159.4	115.8	257	207.9	151.1
18	14.6	10.6	78	63.1	45.8	138	111.6	81.1	198	160.2	116.4	258	208.7	151.6
19	15.4	11.2	79	63.9	46.4	139	112.5	81.7	199	161.0	117.0	259	209.5	152.2
20	16.2	11.8	80	64.7	47.0	140	113.3	82.3	200	161.8	117.6	260	210.3	152.8
21	17.0	12.3	81	65.5	47.6	141	114.1	82.9	201	162.6	118.1	261	211.2	153.4
22	17.8	12.9	82	66.3	48.2	142	114.9	83.5	202	163.4	118.7	262	212.0	154.0
23	18.6	13.5	83	67.1	48.8	143	115.7	84.1	203	164.2	119.3	263	212.8	154.6
24	19.4	14.1	84	68.0	49.4	144	116.5	84.6	204	165.0	119.9	264	213.6	155.2
25	20.2	14.7	85	68.8	50.0	145	117.3	85.2	205	165.8	120.5	265	214.4	155.8
26	21.0	15.3	86	69.6	50.5	146	118.1	85.8	206	166.7	121.1	266	215.2	156.4
27	21.8	15.9	87	70.4	51.1	147	118.9	86.4	207	167.5	121.7	267	216.0	156.9
28	22.7	16.5	88	71.2	51.7	148	119.7	87.0	208	168.3	122.3	268	216.8	157.5
29	23.5	17.0	89	72.0	52.3	149	120.5	87.6	209	169.1	122.8	269	217.6	158.1
30	24.3	17.6	90	72.8	52.9	150	121.4	88.2	210	169.9	123.4	270	218.4	158.7
31	25.1	18.2	91	73.6	53.5	151	122.2	88.8	211	170.7	124.0	271	219.2	159.3
32	25.9	18.8	92	74.4	54.1	152	123.0	89.3	212	171.5	124.6	272	220.1	159.9
33	26.7	19.4	93	75.2	54.7	153	123.8	89.9	213	172.3	125.2	273	220.9	160.5
34	27.5	20.0	94	76.0	55.3	154	124.6	90.5	214	173.1	125.8	274	221.7	161.1
35	28.3	20.6	95	76.9	55.8	155	125.4	91.1	215	173.9	126.4	275	222.5	161.6
36	29.1	21.2	96	77.7	56.4	156	126.2	91.7	216	174.7	127.0	276	223.3	162.2
37	29.9	21.7	97	78.5	57.0	157	127.0	92.3	217	175.6	127.5	277	224.1	162.8
38	30.7	22.3	98	79.3	57.6	158	127.8	92.9	218	176.4	128.1	278	224.9	163.4
39	31.6	22.9	99	80.1	58.2	159	128.6	93.5	219	177.2	128.7	279	225.7	164.0
40	32.4	23.5	100	80.9	58.8	160	129.4	94.0	220	178.0	129.3	280	226.5	164.6
41	33.2	24.1	101	81.7	59.4	161	130.3	94.6	221	178.8	129.9	281	227.3	165.2
42	34.0	24.7	102	82.5	60.0	162	131.1	95.2	222	179.6	130.5	282	228.1	165.8
43	34.8	25.3	103	83.3	60.5	163	131.9	95.8	223	180.4	131.1	283	229.0	166.3
44	35.6	25.9	104	84.1	61.1	164	132.7	96.4	224	181.2	131.7	284	229.8	166.9
45	36.4	26.5	105	84.9	61.7	165	133.5	97.0	225	182.0	132.3	285	230.6	167.5
46	37.2	27.0	106	85.8	62.3	166	134.3	97.6	226	182.8	132.8	286	231.4	168.1
47	38.0	27.6	107	86.6	62.9	167	135.1	98.2	227	183.6	133.4	287	232.2	168.7
48	38.8	28.2	108	87.4	63.5	168	135.9	98.7	228	184.5	134.0	288	233.0	169.3
49	39.6	28.8	109	88.2	64.1	169	136.7	99.3	229	185.3	134.6	289	233.8	169.9
50	40.5	29.4	110	89.0	64.7	170	137.5	99.9	230	186.1	135.2	290	234.6	170.5
51	41.3	30.0	111	89.8	65.2	171	138.3	100.5	231	186.9	135.8	291	235.4	171.0
52	42.1	30.6	112	90.6	65.8	172	139.2	101.1	232	187.7	136.4	292	236.2	171.6
53	42.9	31.2	113	91.4	66.4	173	140.0	101.7	233	188.5	137.0	293	237.0	172.2
54	43.7	31.7	114	92.2	67.0	174	140.8	102.3	234	189.3	137.5	294	237.9	172.8
55	44.5	32.3	115	93.0	67.6	175	141.6	102.9	235	190.1	138.1	295	238.7	173.4
56	45.3	32.9	116	93.8	68.2	176	142.4	103.5	236	190.9	138.7	296	239.5	174.0
57	46.1	33.5	117	94.7	68.8	177	143.2	104.0	237	191.7	139.3	297	240.3	174.6
58	46.9	34.1	118	95.5	69.4	178	144.0	104.6	238	192.5	139.9	298	241.1	175.2
59	47.7	34.7	119	96.3	69.9	179	144.8	105.2	239	193.4	140.5	299	241.9	175.7
60	48.5	35.3	120	97.1	70.5	180	145.6	105.8	240	194.2	141.1	300	242.7	176.3
Hyp.	Opp.	Adj.	Hyp.	Opp.	Adj.	Hyp.	Opp.	Adj.	Hyp.	Opp.	Adj.	Hyp.	Opp.	Adj.
Dist.	Dep.	D. Lat.	Dist.	Dep.	D. Lat.	Dist.	Dep.	D. Lat.	Dist.	Dep.	D. Lat.	Dist.	Dep.	D. Lat.
D Lon		Dep	D Lon		Dep	D Lon		Dep	D Lon		Dep	D Lon		Dep

54° | | | **54°**

Fig 119. A page from Burton's Nautical Tables Tables giving the traverse table for 36° or 54°.

193

Note Carefully.

D. Lat. (difference in lat.) is minutes of latitude which are the same as miles, BUT

Dep. (departure E or W) is miles, but *not* minutes of longitude.

We have now found the movement in a N or S direction, the D.Lat. in miles which are the same as minutes of latitude, and the movement in an E or W direction in Departure, which is in MILES.

Notice that the Traverse Tables have pages headed 1° to 45° at the top, and the same pages are numbered with 89° to 45° at the foot. If the course angle appears at the foot of a page (e.g. 54°), then we must use the captions at the *bottom* of the columns. These now read 'Dist.–Dep.–D.Lat.' (a different sequence from the top headings).

e.g. Co 54° Distance 36 M = D. lat. 21·2 M Dep 29·1 M.

As the Tables are only printed for 1° to 89° all courses should be converted into quadrantal notation. (See Burton's Tables). This also ensures we give the D.Lat. and Dep. the correct Names (N or S, E or W)—

e.g. Co 039° = N 39° E
125° = S 55° E (180 – 125 = 55)
224° = S 44° W (224 – 180 = 44)
293° = N 67° W (360 – 293 = 67)

We can now 'name' the D. Lat. and Dep. the same as course—viz: D. Lat. 21'.2 N Dep. 29·1 miles E.

We must now convert the E or W miles (Dep.) into minutes of longitude in our particular latitude, remembering that the relationship between miles and minutes of longitude depends on the *latitude* we are in. The same Traverse Tables solve this also.

We now use the *latitude* to determine the page, and now we disregard the captions 'Dist.–D.Lat.–

and Dep.', and use the ITALICS captions '*D.Lon.–Dep.*'. Again, if the lat.° are found at the foot of a page, use *italics* captions at foot of column, e.g.:

In Lat. 36°N (or S) Dep. 29·1 M = D. Long. 36'·0 (minutes of longitude)
54° N (or S) Dep. 17·0 M = D. Long. 29'·0

In the Traverse Table page for 54° we should find that against our Dep. 5·9 M its D. Lon. is given as 10'·0 longitude.

We can now re-state the work.

Run Co. 036° = N 36° E 10M
D. Lat.   0°08'·1 N
Dep. 5·9 M in Mean Lat. 54° =
D. Lon.   0°10'·0 E

If the change in latitude (D. Lat.) is large, e.g. we start in latitude 48° and finish in latitude 50°, then we use the Mean Lat., the approximate middle, in that case 49°, for converting the Dep. into D. Lon. A complete example would look like Fig 120a which can be checked with the Traverse Table extract given.

Note that the Names of the D. Lat. and D. Lon. (S and W) must be the same as the quadrantal name of the course (*S 61° W*). The correctness of the conversion from, e.g. 234° to S 54° W, can be checked by consulting the diagram on each right hand Traverse Table page which, in our example would show

306°	054°
→ 234°	126°

Note also that the 'summing up' of the figures follows the usual algebraic system—when names are the same (W and W lon.) add; when names are opposite (N and S lat.) subtract the smaller from the larger and name as the larger, (N).

Where a number of different courses are involved, the D. Lat. and departure of each must

Old EP (or starting point)	36°05'·0 N	24°40'·0 W
Run 24 M on Co 234° T = S 54° W		
D. Lat. =	14'·1 S	
Dep. 19·4 M, in Mean Lat. 36°		
D. Lon. =		24'·0 W
New EP	35°50'·9 N	25°04'·0 W

Fig 120a.

Last EP 45°20'·0 N 18°40'·0 W.

Course	Distance	D. Lat.		Dep.	
		N	S	W	E
050° = N 50° E	24 miles	15·4			18·4
340° = N 20° W	30 miles	28·2		10·3	
075° = N 75° E	42 miles	10·9			40·6
350° = N 10° W	18 miles	17·7		3·1	
095° = S 85° E	12 miles		1·0		12·0
015° = N 15° E	36 miles	34·8			9·3
Tidal stream setting					
241° = S 61° W	2 kn × 18 hrs = 36 M		17·5	31·5	
249° = S 69° W	1½ kn × 6 hrs = 9M		3·2	8·4	
		107·0	21·7	53·3	80·3
		−21·7			−53·3
	D. Lat.	85'·3 N		Dep	27·0 E

Last EP		45°20'·0 N	18°40'·0 W
D. Lat. 85'·3 N =	1°25'·3 N	
Dep. 27·0 E in M. Lat. 46°		
D. Lon. =		38'·9 E
New EP	46°45'·3 N	18°01'·1 W

Fig 120b.

be turned up and listed, but it is not necessary to convert each Dep. into D. Lon. separately.
The Deps can be summed up and the total (net) Dep. converted into a total D. Lon. Note also that one or a series of tidal streams can be treated in the same way and much work saved. The secret lies in a clear, methodical tabulation, as in Fig 120b.

Note that for conversion of the Departure into D. Lon. a Mean Lat. of 46° has been used as this is about halfway between 45°20′ N and 46°45′.3 N. (The exact figure is of course

$$45°20 + \frac{1°25·3}{2} = 46°03', \text{ but exact}$$

interpolation is seldom necessary).

It would have been tedious to have plotted all these courses and tidal streams on a chart, and slight inaccuracies would be probable. The use of traverse tables for this type of problem will give a more accurate answer—indeed it will be as accurate as the courses and distances used correspond with those actually sailed.

The traverse tables can be used for the solution of a number of similar problems, for example, to find the course and distance between two positions of known latitude and longitude.

e.g.
What is the true course and distance from a position 36°14′ N 28°20′ W to a position 35°40′ N 29°18′ W?

First position	36°14′ N	28°20′ W
Second position	35°40′ N	29°18′ W
D. Lat.	34′ S	
D. Lon.		58′ W
In Mean Lat. 36° dep. =		46.9 M

D. Lat. 34′.1 and Dep. 46.9 are found on Traverse Table for 54°, against distance 58 miles. S 54° W (names same as D. Lat. and D. Lon.) = 234° T.

Answer: Course 234° T, Distance 58 miles.

The Tables are based on the solution of a *plane* right-angled triangle. While the answers given are sufficiently accurate for a relatively small triangle when distances above about 600 miles are involved accuracy falls off and the problem requires the solution of a spherical triangle. For distances above this figure the table of meridional parts can be used, but as this has little practical application for coastal and short sea passages it is not dealt with here.

18. Celestial Navigation

In celestial or astro navigation the yacht's position is established using heavenly bodies instead of terrestrial objects. When within sight of identifiable objects on land, a position line established by a bearing (or a vertical sextant angle) of a single object, or a fix by bearings, horizontal sextant angles or VSA's of two or more such objects will give the most accurate result. When out of sight of land, various radio methods of position finding may be available, but accuracy decreases with distance from the station, and (except with the most sophisticated equipment) they are valueless in mid-ocean. If any heavenly body and the horizon can be seen anywhere in the world a position line can be established within 10–15 minutes. Accuracy to within 10 miles is possible under rough conditions, and to within 2 miles under moderate to favourable conditions.

By day, the sun, often the moon, and occasionally a planet can be used. Moon, planets and stars can be used at twilight, and under very favourable conditions of light can also be used in darkness. The body must of course be visible, either in a clear sky or through gaps in clouds.

No higher mathematics are involved: simple straightforward formulae are used which anyone can soon master. Taking sights with a sextant needs practice but tolerable accuracy should be possible after an hour or so. The rapid sight reduction tables now available (referred to later) simplify the calculations immensely.

Exactly as with sights from terrestrial objects, a single observation of a single heavenly body will provide only a position *line*, somewhere on which is the observer's position. To obtain an 'observed position' (so called to distinguish it from a fix obtained by terrestrial objects), it is necessary (Fig 121.) either to observe two (or more) heavenly bodies (almost) simultaneously, or to observe one body (usually the sun), then to proceed until the body's position in the sky has materially moved when a second observation is taken. The second position line should make a wide angle to the first (ideally about 90°). The first position line is transferred forward in the direction and distance the yacht has sailed since the first observation was taken. (Fig 122.) This is precisely analogous to the 'running fix'.

Some navigators use the sun exclusively, since this is the easiest and most frequently visible. The ability to shoot the moon, planets and stars is an advantage, as it enables an observed position to be found at once without having to wait for a second sight after a run of some hours, as must be done if only the sun is used. If three (or more) heavenly bodies are observed (nearly) simultaneously, the position line given by each should theoretically cross all others at a point. As with compass bearings of three or more terrestrial objects they seldom do so, but form a 'cocked hat', the size of which gives a good guide as to the accuracy of the sights. (Fig 123.)

Ocean passages

A large yacht, sail or power, equipped with the latest hyperbolic radio position finding equipment, could cross an ocean and make a good landfall without taking a celestial observation. Without such equipment, an ocean-going yachtsman must be capable of taking celestial sights. It is interesting to note that many captains of passenger liners insist on their watch-keeping officers taking celestial sights daily and on the ship's position being checked in spite of the ship using the very latest radio and other devices which pin-point the position exactly. This is partly to keep the watch-keeping officers 'in training', and partly to ensure the radio fixing equipment is working correctly.

For these reasons it is fair to say that any yacht however well equipped, should have the means and skill aboard to enable accurate fixes by sextant observations of celestial bodies to be made, if it is proposed to make an ocean passage.

Long-distance semi-coastal passages

Here we are considering such passages as between England and Gibraltar, Malta and Crete, Falmouth and Cork (Ireland), Scotland and Denmark, San Francisco and Vancouver. These passages have often been safely made without the use of celestial navigation. Radio beacons can be used at various points (but by no means at all stages of the passage), and careful working up of the position by dead reckoning can be employed. However, the EP can be seriously in error— perhaps dangerously so—if for any reason a fix by DF beacons or by observations of land objects cannot be established for several days. This could

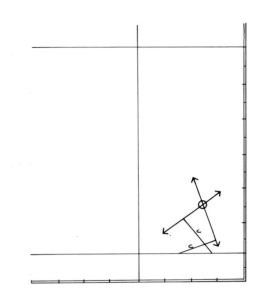

Fig 121. Two simultaneous sights: moon and one star. Construction line (c) is actual bearing to celestial body. Position line is at right angles to it.

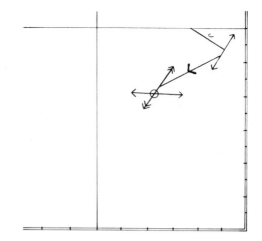

occur if the yacht were obliged to lie a-hull in heavy weather, or had engine trouble, or the radio became unserviceable. If fixes by land objects are being relied upon there is a tendency for the course to be laid perhaps imprudently close inshore. If there is any risk of heavy weather a yacht is safest well off-shore. An offing of 50 miles is none too great if the coast is liable to be a lee shore, bearing in mind that a yacht lying a-hull may drift downwind at 1 kn or more.

The ability to take celestial sights encourages the setting of a course well offshore, with the knowledge that the position can probably be observed at frequent intervals only dependent on visibility of the sun or any other heavenly body. Celestial sights taken 50 or more miles from the shore should provide more accurate positions than any taken from radio beacons.

Short coastal or sea passages

Celestial sights are seldom necessary on short coastal passages, taking only up to perhaps 36 hours. Nevertheless, occasions do arise when a celestial observation can be of real value. On

Fig 122.   Two sun sights, but with a run of 20 miles 240° between them. The position (top right) has been transferred to double arrowed line to give intersection which is position.

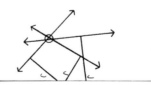

Fig 123.   Three simultaneous sights. Each position line is obtained from a different star: they intersect to give an observed position.

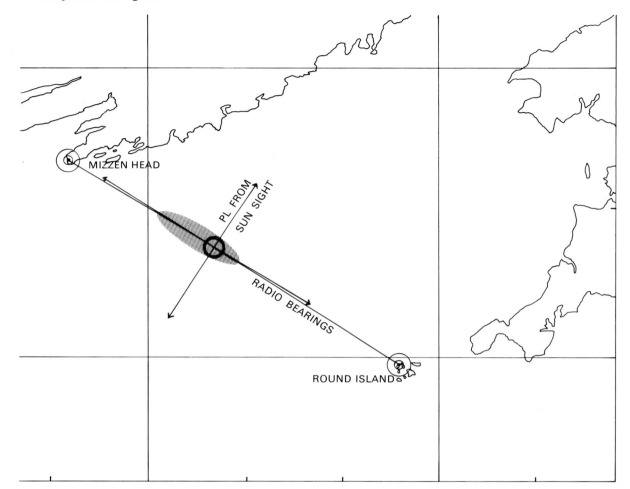

Fig 124. Crossing DF bearings with a celestial observation. The DF stations at Mizzen Head and Round Island are so much in line with yacht's position that she is only known to be in shaded area. But when crossed by position line from morning sun sight, a fix is obtained in red circle.

a passage from the south coast of England to France (say Cherbourg), one may have a slow passage and be very glad to be able to establish one's position while well out of sight of land. The crossing from Land's End to southern Ireland (say the Fastnet Rock lighthouse) is about 180 miles. There is a good RDF station ahead (at Mizzen Head) and another nearly astern (Round Island) but DF stations abeam (needed to establish the position along the track line) are too far off to be of value. A celestial observation along this line can be of great help. (Fig 124.)

Apart from the occasions—admittedly infrequent—where celestial observations are of value when coastal passage making, the knowledge that such sights *can* be taken is itself satisfying and rewarding. No skipper or navigator can claim to be fully competent if he is not able to take, and use, celestial observations.

Accuracy of positions

The accuracy of an observed position will naturally depend first on the experience of the observer, and secondly on the sea conditions and size of the yacht. As a broad guide, the average 'week-end' yachtsman in a 10 m sailing yacht in a moderate sea, say, up to Beaufort force 4 or 5, should obtain a position line to within 5 miles. A practised yachtsman should get equal accuracy up to force 7 if the sky is clear. These are conservative figures. I have taken sun sights from a known position (near a landfall buoy) to within 1 mile in a 10 m yacht in force 5 while singlehanded.

The only essential equipment needed for celestial sights is:
(a) A sextant.
(b) A deck watch or chronometer, or good timepiece and radio.
(c) A nautical almanac and table book.

The alternative combinations are:

    (a) Almanac for current year—Nautical almanac
        Navigational Tables—Burton's or Norie's,
or (b) Almanac for current year— Sight Reduction Tables— for Air. AP3270 or HO249; or Admiralty NP401 or HO229
or (c) Reeds' Nautical Almanac for current year.

If you want to know whether to study celestial navigation remember:

1. The ability to take celestial observations is essential for ocean passages, desirable for short passages, interesting and adds a new dimension to open-water sailing.
2. The most expensive item required is a good timepiece. If a radio capable of picking up time signals is aboard, a good watch can be used. The only other items for celestial work are books as mentioned and a sextant, which will not be costly if one of the plastic type (such as the Ebbco) is used.
3. Celestial Navigation is not difficult; there is no 'black magic' about it. There is less to learn than in coastal navigation. There are many good text books on the subject, and many courses and classes are available. Uniform with this volume, is *Ocean Yacht Navigator* by the same author which fully covers celestial navigation.

19. Certificates for the yacht navigator

This book has more than covered what is required for the navigational part of the Royal Yachting Association Yachtmaster Offshore Certificate. This is the official British certificate of competency for sailors and is co-sponsored by the Department of Transport. Only the Yachtmaster Ocean is more advanced and comprises the addition of celestial sights and proved record of navigating by them (covered and explained in *Ocean Yacht Navigator* by Kenneth Wilkes).

The RYA training scheme in respect of habitable sailing yachts is now at five levels (there are also motor boat and dinghy sailing certificates). These are Competent Crew, Day Skipper/Watch Leader, Coastal Skipper, Yachtmaster Offshore and Yachtmaster Ocean. The coastal skipper is expected to have 'the knowledge to skipper a cruising yacht on coastal cruises, but does not necessarily have the experience needed to undertake longer passages'. The yachtmaster offshore is 'an experienced yachtsman, competent to skipper a cruising yacht on any passage which can be completed without the use of astro-navigation'. The definitions are inevitably a little unprecise in the world of sailing which is undertaken for fun and sport anyway; a very long voyage can now be undertaken using satellite navigation and no astro sights, but one can see what the RYA is trying to put over.

The official booklet for the yachtmaster offshore examination is 'Royal Yachting Association national cruising scheme (sail) syllabus and log book—G 15. This shows what is needed for each examination and incorporates a log for the candidate to record his qualifying sea time. (RYA booklet G 18 is a very similar scheme for motor boat skippers and navigators and much of the same navigation applies).

From the syllabus it will be seen that navigation forms the greatest part of the course of instruction on shore. Other parts comprise signals, meteorology, safety, 'seagoing practices' and the rules for prevention of collision at sea.

The certificate of competence is awarded after a practical examination at sea in a yacht no less than 24 feet overall length. This can last from eight to twelve hours with the examiner posing practical problems, but also theoretical ones, supposed marks or navigational situations, which nevertheless the candidate will have to go to the chart table or use navigational instruments or drills to solve.

There is a shore based course especially important in navigation because an intermediate certificate is awarded for 'satisfactory completion of a course of instruction'. Papers to round off such courses are on chart work, dead reckoning navigation, pilotage into harbour, position fixing, tides and tidal streams, passage planning, the magnetic compass and other essential instruments. Obviously from time to time there are amendments and additions and the latest copy of G 15 (or G 18) should be consulted.

Here is the yachtmaster syllabus as it applies to navigation only:

Subject	Subdivision	Refer to Chapter in Practical Yacht Navigator
Definition of position, course and speed	1. Latitude and longitude	2
	2. Knowledge of standard terms	6
	3. True bearings and courses	1
	4. The knot	1
Navigational drawing instruments	1. Parallel rulers	3
	2. Dividers and compasses	3
	3. Proprietary plotting instruments	3
Navigational charts and publications	1. Suppliers—Admiralty, Stanford etc	2
	2. Information shown on Admiralty charts	2
	3. Chart symbols—Chart 5011	2
	4. Standard chartwork	2
	5. Projections-Mercator and gnomonic	2
	6. Navigational publications in common use	2
	7. Chart correction	2
Dead reckoning and Estimated Position	1. Definition of DR and EP	7
	2. Working up DR and EP by plotting on a chart	7
The position line	1. Sources of position lines	9
The magnetic compass	1. Allowance for variation. Change of variation with time and position	5
	2. Siting of compass and causes of deviation	5
	3. Deviation. Allowance for	5
	4. Steering and hand bearing compasses	3, 4, 5
	5. Swing for deviation (but not correction)	5
Position fixing	1. Techniques of visual fixing	9
	2. Horizontal angle fixing	9
	3. Running fixes	9
	4. Radio fixes	4, 10
	5. Fixes containing a mixture of position lines	9
	6. Derivation of position from a line of soundings	9
	7. Ranges by dipping distances	9
Basic Coastal Navigation	1. Routine for navigating a yacht in coastal waters	14
	2. Strategy of course laying	7
Tides	1. Causes of tides—springs and neaps	8
	2. Tide tables—Admiralty and yachtsmen's almanacs	8
	3. Tidal levels and datums	8
	4. Times and heights at standard ports	8
	5. The rule of twelfths	8
	6. Corrections for secondary ports	8
	7. Tidal anomalies (Solent, etc.)	8
Tidal Streams	1. Tidal stream atlas	8
	2. Tidal diamonds	8
	3. Tidal stream information in sailing directions and yachtsmen's almanacs	8
	4. Allowance for tidal streams in computing a course to steer	8
	5. Tide rips, overfalls and races	8
	6. Tidal stream observation by buoys, beacons etc	8
Buoyage	1. IALA system buoyage in Region A	2
	2. Limitations of buoys as navigational aids	2
Lights	1. Characteristics	2, 9
	2. Ranges—Visual, luminous and nominal ranges	9
	3. Light lists—Admiralty and in yachtsmen's almanacs	2
Echo sounders and lead line	1. Principle of operation	3
	2. Types available—rotating dial and pointer, recording	3
	3. Reduction of soundings	3
	4. 'Second trace' echoes	3
	5. Marking of lead line	8
Radio direction finding	1. Radio beacons, ALRS Vol. II and yachtsmen's almanacs	4
	2. D/F receivers, types of aerials, method of operation, audio and	4

Thanks are due to John Driscoll, National Sailing Coach, RYA, for help in compiling this chapter.

Index